I Know What Heaven Looks Like

A Modern Day Coming of Age Story

By Lawrence T. Richardson

I wrote this book for several reasons and for several people, most especially, *me*.

–Lawrence

Table of Contents

Acknowledgements

A special thanks to God for the light, love, and power within me that sustains all my endeavors.

A special thanks to Linden Hills United Church of Christ for being a space of love and community during the process of writing this book.

A special thanks to the late, Leelah Alcorn for waking me up.

Thank you for believing in me, praying for me, giving me a chance, and encouraging me—whether you know it or not, you have contributed greatly to my journey: *Noah Alvarez; Renaé Antalan; Black Transmen Inc.; Jay Bakker; Oby Ballinger; Marc Blakesley; Lisa Bodenheim; Sarah Boua; Brown Boi Project; Marie Claire Buckley; Delna Buhariwalla; Janet Bystrom; Center for Progressive Renewal; Denise Chan; Gabrielle Civil; Rae Cornelius; K. M. Davis; Aaron Dreyling; Andrew Dugstad; Shernell Edney; Yvette Flunder; Emily Goldthwaite Fries; Roshee and Destiny Cryer-Greene; Kim Higgs; Malcolm Himschoot; Eliot Howard; Jo Hudson; Kathryn Matthews Huey; Gloria Irvin; Devoria Jackson; Amy and Craig Jarrell; Deborah Johnson; Micah King; Charlotte Landreau; Talisha, Jean and Meeya Lormeus; Natalie and Rob Lucken; Ashley Marcus; Danna McCutcheon; Kenneth McKinnis Jr; Rakeal McKinnis; Minnesota Trans Health Coalition; ChanSoon Olson; Elena Pettis Larssen; NGLI Class of 2028; Jennifer Pritchett; Dawan and Sherise Propps; Josh and Melissa Rensch; Betty Richardson; Cassandra Richardson; Joyce Richardson; Minnie Richardson; Racine Richardson; Robert Richardson; Nathan Roberts; Jeremiah Satterthwaite; David Schoen; Karen Smith*

Sellers; John Sellner; Vanessa Sodd; Enzi Tanner; Deborah Thorp; Cameron Trimble; United Church of Christ; Velma Wagner; Rex Wiederanders; Sara Wilcox; Camolly Williams; Angela Wilson; Oprah Winfrey; Julie Young.

Part 1. I Am No Ordinary Man

Chapter 1: My Earliest Memories

I am a man. But I am no ordinary man. Growing up, I was a skinny, caramel colored kid with wide, brown eyes and a Jheri Curl afro living in predominantly white Midwestern neighborhoods in the 1980s. In the summers, I played with neighborhood kids—building forts and devising plans to make money for food and treats, oftentimes topless and shoeless, wearing frayed jean shorts that were previously pants that had been cut off at the knees when my legs became too long for them.

During the school year, I lived with my mother, and I spent the weekends and the summers at my paternal grandmother's house. One day, during a summer visit to my grandmother's house, I fell asleep and dreamed the most peculiar dream. In the dream, my spindly, 7-year-old self was transformed into a tall and broad man of 40-something. Big, round, shoulders; a bright smile; and wearing a preacher's robe standing at a pulpit.

After the image of myself as a wise-eyed minister danced through my mind, I startled awake and immediately felt inspired to organize my first church service—something that I had never done nor desired to do before this dream.

I ran to the painted white, aluminum shed in the backyard of my grandmother's tiny, red-trimmed white house. She lived near the river in a semi-developed, industrial neighborhood. In the shed where she kept all her gardening and yard equipment, I spotted the brown, plastic milk crate that was used to carry the collard greens, rhubarb, raspberries and green beans my grandmother grew in the backyard. I emptied the dirt that was left behind in the crate onto the unmowed lawn and dragged it to the back porch. A thin, dusty brown carpet covered the always creaking floorboards and I determined that this was the perfect place to use as a sanctuary.

An old, silver and black boom box was retrieved from inside the house, plugged into the wall, and placed next to the milk crate on the floor. The antenna of the boom box, which was fastened to itself by duct tape, had begun to slide and the sounds coming through the speakers were muffled at best.

My grandmother co-owned a soul food restaurant that had recently closed because it was no longer profitable, so she decided to store some of the leftover restaurant furniture and equipment in the basement to have on hand for future catering jobs. I retrieved six chairs from the basement and arranged them into a semicircle facing the boom box and milk crate.

The computer manufacturing company where my grandmother also worked for 35 years was behind the house—on the other side of the alley. We were the only Black family on the block at the time, so my grandmother warned us to be careful. Except for next door neighbor, Cathy, who helped us plant raspberry bushes and came by to talk to my grandmother from time to time, it was a rule that no one from the neighborhood could come into the house. I was left so invigorated by my dream that I disregarded the rule of no company and went outside to solicit the neighbors' participation for my church service.

"Excuse me, I am having church at my granny's house and you should come right away!" I knocked hard on the dozen or so doors on our block and spoke politely to the older white neighbors.

Many of the neighbors declined my invitation—saying they weren't interested—but five of them accepted, including Cathy and the man who lived directly across the street from Cathy who was always outside watering his flowers with a green hose. The neighbors followed me up the front steps, through the living room, then through the kitchen onto the back porch. As they sat down in the folding chairs, I turned the knob on the boom box to the Christian radio station and stood on top of the milk crate.

"Thank you all for joining me today. Let us pray, Lord Jesus, thank you for this day. Hallelujah! And thank you for your children. Amen."

I paused so that we could listen to the radio. I couldn't make out the song over the static, and because the faces of those gathered were a mix of relief and confusion, I concluded that they didn't understand the song either. But that didn't discourage me.

When the song finished, and the radio announcer started to speak, I unplugged the boom box and began sharing what was on my heart.

With a big-toothy grin, I lifted my hands and shouted, "Yes, Jesus loves me! Yes, Jesus loves me! Yes, Jesus loves me for the Bible tells me so. Jesus loves us everybody and we should be happy!"

Feeling satisfied, I smiled into the eyes of the captivated neighbors, stepped off the milk crate, waved at them, and ran back outside to play.

****

As excited as I was to play church, I enjoyed going to church equally. The experience of seeing the different people, hearing about God, and being with my grandmother invigorated me and is what made the sometimes 2-hour-long services attractive each week. I would've gone to church even if it wasn't one of my grandmother's rules that we attend church when we stayed with her, because it was the only time during the week that I felt tenderness. The corporate act of surrendering to the movement of a worship service and to the Spirit bonded me emotionally to my grandmother, and we usually got along well because of it.

Minnie Richardson, or Mother Richardson as she was called at church, was a stoic, strong woman who grew her nails until they broke, and kept her hair cropped and curled closely to her head. She wore black, navy or brown slacks with printed button-ups during the week under her long, blue work coat; and at church, she wore long skirts with matching blazers and big Sunday hats.

She was too young to be a grandmother, but her kids had kids when they were kids, and as a result, she became "Mother" to many. Mother Richardson was the kind of woman who could fry chicken and change the oil in a car.

Her father was a southern, Baptist preacher, and when she migrated to the Midwest in the 1960s for better work and housing opportunities, my grandmother didn't veer from the teachings of her youth. She joined a Southern Missionary Baptist church and devoted a significant amount of time, resources, and money to the church.

In her church, people weren't baptized as infants, instead, people are baptized when they are able to publicly declare their faith in God, and because I was able to articulate my passion for God, I was baptized this summer.

I arrived at the church on the day of my baptism with my grandmother in her old, beat up Volkswagen Rabbit that had pieces of cardboard covering the rusted through holes of the floor. We made our way downstairs to the church basement where nearly 2 dozen had gathered in a room and were waiting to get baptized.

I recognized many of the folks from baptism rehearsal the day before. The well-lit room had a chalkboard on the wall, a big oak desk, and walls lined with dusted boxes. I discovered candles and Christmas decorations in the boxes nearest me as I curiously peeked through the tops and carrying holes to entertain myself.

"Alright, everyone we only have a limited time to get dressed. Just as we rehearsed, let's get back here in 10 minutes," a modestly confident, tall and slender woman wearing a long white dress and bright, purple lipstick announced as several of the adults disappeared down the hall to the bathrooms to change their clothes.

I started toward the door.

"Teasha, come back here…where do you think you're going?"

My grandmother reached out her heavy arm and blocked me from moving further. "Take off your clothes," she said. Her brown eyes were serious.

I stood there embarrassed and resenting. I was wearing thick, white tights and a white lace dress that had a pink ribbon sewn around the middle for a belt. My shoes were made of a shiny, white plastic that squeaked when I rubbed my feet together.

I closed my eyes, took off everything as quickly as I could and handed the items to my grandmother. She tucked my clothing items into a nearby paper grocery sack, yanked my arms up and pulled a long, white, cotton gown down along my arms and over my head onto my skinny torso. I reluctantly pressed my lips together and knew not to complain about my clothes.

Children were seen at church, not heard, and because of past conversations with my grandmother on this very topic, I knew no one was interested in hearing about how much I hated wearing girls clothes—especially on the day of my baptism.

After getting dressed, we were escorted up the creaking vinyl stairs to the warm, stained-glass sanctuary with royal red carpet that matched the foam seat cushions draped across the wooden pews. We were welcomed by several hundred black and brown people who were scattered loosely throughout the polished room. As we filed into the 3 rows that were tucked to the right of the pulpit, my attention and heartbeat relaxed into the choir's gospel tune.

> *Wade in the water*
> *Wade in the water, children,*
> *Wade in the water*
> *God's a-going to trouble the water...*

I had never seen a baptism before but during rehearsal I learned that the preacher was going to dunk me into the bathtub-sized pool and then, when he brought me back out of the water, I would be a member of God's holy family and my sins would be washed away. I didn't understand the concept of sin at the time, but God was very important to me and I was excited about being a part of God's family.

When it was time to come forward, I was invited by an usher to stand at the bottom of the stairs that led up to the baptismal pool.

When it was my turn to take the steps toward the pool, I walked up to meet my pastor who helped me climb into the cold water. I felt foolish wearing a gown and standing in a bathtub with my pastor who was also wearing a gown—except his was black and looked slightly heavier than mine.

The pastor positioned me to stand alongside him facing forward, he placed one hand behind my back and one hand on my head.

"By the profession of your faith, I baptize you in the name of the Father, in the name of the Son, and in the name of the Holy Spirit!" My heart raced as he thrusted my body backwards into the water.

I came out of the frigid water to see the arm of an usher extended for me to grab. The usher lifted me out of the tub and guided me down the carpeted steps to my grandmother and one of the other church mothers who were both standing at the bottom of the stairs waiting to cocoon me into a large, white towel.

"Here you go, baby," my grandmother said as she handed me the brown paper bag containing my church clothes.

I dressed quickly once we entered the basement. I didn't feel any different immediately after my baptism, but my skin seemed more sensitive and I was keenly aware of the clothes I was wearing and how ashamed I felt because I couldn't wear slacks and a dress shirt or a suit like other boys at church.

When we returned to the sanctuary it was time for my first communion as a new member of the church—God's family. The preacher who was now dried and wearing an even heavier, white preacher's robe, was standing behind a large wooden table at the front of the room.

The table was covered with brass plates of wafers and stacked brass trays of tiny plastic cups filled with grape juice. After he read the Bible passage commemorating the sacred act and recounting the details from the night Jesus shared a similar meal with his friends, the preacher held up one tray and one plate and handed the dishes to the communion assistants who were now lined up at the table waiting to receive the elements that they would distribute among the congregation.

Let us break bread together, on our knees... The choir erupted in song and the band began to play. When the trays passed my grandmother and me, she picked up two cups and a wafer, and instructed me to get a wafer as well.

"I'll hold your juice so that you don't spill any of it on your pretty dress," she whispered loudly over the music. "Now this represents the blood of our Lord and Savior Jesus Christ that was shed on Calvary." She lifted the cups in the air.

"What's this for?" I asked, thrusting my wafer in the air trying to mimic her. The small circle was hard and felt like cardboard.

"This represents the body of our Lord and Savior Jesus Christ that was broken for us on Calvary!" She proudly raised her wafer in the air and smiled down at me.

Fascinated by the tiny cross that was embossed upon it, I yelled, "Why does it have a T on it?"

"Shush...not so loud. That's the cross on Calvary where Jesus hung his head and died for you and me. Every time you eat this, remember Jesus!" she said.

My grandmother turned her attention away from me and joined the others who were singing.

Let us drink wine together, on our knees…

I sat back in the pew and studied the wafer in my hand. I pressed my thumb into the center of the wafer and broke it into even tinier pieces wondering how many times Christ's body could be broken up. A few moments later, my grandmother leaned down and said, "You need to eat the wafer before you can drink the juice."

She didn't explain why, and she hadn't noticed my destruction of the body, but as I saw her put the tiny cup to her lips and consume its contents, I quickly scraped up the wafer pieces into my hand that were formed into a little mountain on the pew cushion next to me. I scooped the pieces into my mouth, stood up, and extended my hand to receive my cup from my grandmother. I braced myself against the back of the pew in front of us and leaned my head back. My lips puckered as my mouth filled with the tangy sweetness and I wondered if Jesus' blood really tasted like grapes.

"You may be seated," the pastor announced. "Let us now prepare to hear the word of God."

We returned to our seats and passed the emptied cups down the aisle to be collected. "Thanks be to God," we responded in unison.

The musicians began to play again, this time, to transition us further along the order of worship to the scripture reading that happened just before the preacher began his sermon.

My agitation with my clothes quietly continued.

I arrived at church that day with one pair of panties, and since I left them on during the baptism, they were wet and had to be taken off before I put back on my dress clothes. I squirmed around in the pew picking at my tights, thinking that if I could shift them, I'd feel some relief.

"Settle down now," my grandmother whispered as she pinched a small piece of my arm flesh between her thumb and index finger. She enjoyed my interest in church, but she also enjoyed this time for her own relief. As she surrendered to the Spirit, her arms flung up overhead and she greeted the pastor's presence at the podium with, "Amen."

I crawled under the pew like I usually did when I was bored, exploring, or agitated, and I laid back on the carpeted floor. The idea returned to shift my tights, and this time as my fingertips reached down to lift the hot, stretchy material from my skin, I felt a tingling sensation that I had never felt before that day. A subtle piercing traveled along my legs and deep into my loins. The surge of energy felt good.

I traced and retraced the entire seam of my tights, and each time, faster than before. The excitement happening deep within me increased and a volt of energy charged to the space gathered at my thighs. I picked loose the stitch between my legs until all that was left was an open hole that exposed my genitals.

I stared down at myself. Granny always called it a "monkey" and I called it "down there". To understand the sensations that were happening "down there", I began to trace the brown mass of flesh with my fingers similarly to the way I had been tracing the braided seam of my tights.

The tips of my tiny fingers moved up one side and around to the other side, encircling the protrusion that gave me the most pleasure.

My heart beat into my fingers and my legs started to quiver. Just as I threw my head back onto the carpet in ecstasy, one of my older cousins, who was sitting on the pew near my grandmother and me, reached down beneath the seat, slapped my hand and shouted, "You're disgusting!"

"What's so disgusting? This is my body," I quipped. I was as ashamed as any 7-year-old caught masturbating for the first time could be.

I snapped my legs closed, pulled down my dress, and crawled from under the wooden seat. My grandmother, oblivious to my gratification, was now standing and singing along to the gospel choir that erupted at the end of the preacher's message. Confused and breathless, my heart and mind were racing. Where did those tingly feelings come from? Why did my cousin think it was disgusting? Was *I* disgusting?

"That service sure was powerful! God is good," my grandmother said joyfully as we filed out of the sanctuary.

We made our way down the large concrete staircase, onto the sidewalk and into her car that was parked a block and a half away. "And you're going to heaven now, Teasha; how do you feel?" she asked.

I climbed into the backseat and she straightened the rearview mirror to look at me. I didn't have the words to describe all that I was feeling in that moment and I wasn't sure I should tell her about what happened under the pew, so I shrugged my shoulders and replied, "I don't know."

The remainder of the car ride home was silent, and I stared out the window as thoughts of the day and snapshots of the neighborhood passed like mile markers on a highway.

When we returned to my grandmother's house, I flung off those uncomfortable clothes leaving a trail of the day's garments from the front door to the hamper in the bathroom. From the hamper, I retrieved a pair of shorts, some underwear and a single sock. I put on the underwear and then slipped into the shorts. I rolled up the sock into a ball and then placed it in my underwear.

It had been several months since I'd started secretly sleeping with a rolled-up sock in my underwear. I thought it would help my penis grow in. I sunk down into the pile of pillows and blankets that was my bed on my grandmother's living room floor, staring at the cotton mound in my shorts thinking. *Did the tingling happen because I was now baptized? Why did my cousin call me disgusting? Would I have to wear girl's church clothes when my body was done growing?*

****

"Granny, how can I start my own business, so I can get more money?" I asked my grandmother one afternoon. It hadn't occurred to me then to tell her why I needed more money.

"You need a product. People will only give you money if you produce something for them. I have my food and I have my hands. I use my hands at work to solder the motherboards for the computers they sell, and I sell my food to people who want the best southern cooking in town." She smiled and untied her apron, then collapsed onto her brown, polyester recliner with an exhausted look.

"How do I find a product?" I insisted.

"Use your mind. What do you like to do and what is right in front of you? Use your mind. Now chile let me close my eyes for a while," she said.

My grandmother stretched back far enough into the chair that the footrest lifted. She closed her eyes and the lines on her caramel-colored forehead eventually relaxed. I stood watching until her breathing slowed down, her full lips slightly parted, and she nodded off to sleep.

As granny slept, I took the pins and ponytail out of my hair and changed into some shorts. My aunt who was babysitting left; my sister, Tanya, and little cousins were outback playing in the yard; and my teenage cousin, Joyce, who lived with my grandmother permanently, was in her bedroom listening to music.

'What do you like to do and what is right in front of you?' played over and over in my mind. I started my search for product in the basement where my grandmother kept her catering supplies.

Giant pans stacked high, boxes of Styrofoam cups to the ceiling, metal folding chairs, and food warming units were among the items packed neatly into the small, unfinished room that smelled like mothballs in a stuffy warehouse. I discovered a large box that contained several small boxes of stir stick straws. I was filled with excitement because I really like drinking through straws.

I took one of the boxes of straws upstairs to the kitchen and emptied them onto the counter. There were too many to count and I kept losing my place, so I grouped them into piles of 10. I had 10 piles of 10. I opened the drawer and found several twist-ties and tried tying one of them around the bundle of straws, but the bundle was too wide. So, I ran to Joyce's room and knocked on her door.

"Joyce can I have some of your rubber binders?"

"What rubber binders?" She opened the door annoyed at me.

"The ones you use for your hair. I only need 10."

"10? You trying to take all my stuff!" she said loudly over the crackly R&B music coming from her broken boombox.

"Come on, please? Please Joyce! Let me just have 10. I know you have a whole bunch because I saw them when granny did my hair," I cried.

"Fine! Stop whining like a little baby. God!" she said, walking across the narrow room to her oversized chest of drawers. "What do you need them for anyway?"

"I need them for my product."

"Whatever! And don't wake up granny running through here like that," she said. She then counted out 10 hair binders and placed them into my eager hand.

"Thanks, Joyce!" I said, trying to contain my excitement. I ran out of her room and she closed the door behind me.

I wrapped a rubber binder around each bundle of straws and ran outside to my neighbors with the 10 bundles of straws in hand.

No one answered the doors of the first set of single-family houses I went to across the street, which left me discouraged, so I went to Cathy's white house with red shutters next door.

Cathy was always friendly and if anyone was going to support my new idea, I knew she would. I knocked hard, and when she answered the door, my elation was palpable.

"Cathy, will you buy my product? I'm trying to make $100," I said, beaming.

Cathy had shoulder-length, curly blonde hair. She often wore jeans that were pulled up high around her waist. She always smiled and looked at you in the eyes when she spoke. Every time she was outside, she always had several cats following her around her yard. Granny told me that all those cats lived in Cathy's house which was so hard for me to imagine because my mother was against us having animals living with us.

"I don't have $100 but I do have $1," Cathy said, reaching into her pocket for the $1 bill. She took one of the bundles from my hand and tucked the dollar into the front pocket of my shorts.

"Thanks, Cathy!" I said, excitedly. My face was bright, and my eyes were brighter. Cathy smiled at me, picked up one of the cats that was now crawling around her feet, and closed the white, painted door as I pinged down the steps and back onto the sidewalk.

I went down the block and knocked on every door. For those who answered, I told them that I was selling product for $1. After I sold all the straws, I raced back down the street all the way home.

"Granny, granny, wake up!" I cried. I grabbed the arm of the chair and shook her relentlessly.

"What's the matter?" Although her 52-year-old body was tired from the day and lifetime of work, she jumped up out of her chair immediately. "What happened?" she shouted.

"Look!" I began to pick the crumpled dollars from my pockets.

"Where did you get all that money?" she asked, looking simultaneously puzzled and relieved.

"I still have the $10 you gave me, too. I'm rich!" I dropped to the floor and began smoothing out all the bills.

"What did you do?" She started picking up the money from the floor.

"I found some product for the neighbors," I replied, now organizing the dollars.

"What product?"

I didn't look up to meet her gaze, but her voice sounded intrigued, so I responded, "The straws from the basement. Joyce gave me rubber binders and the neighbors gave me $1 for them," I explained.

"Joyce, get in here!" Joyce emerged from her bedroom. "What is Teasha talking about? Straws and rubber bands from the basement?"

"I don't know. Teasha came in here asking for 10 rubber bands and I said not to wake you." Granny headed for the basement and Joyce went back to her room and closed her door.

"You sold these?" I ran into the kitchen to discover my grandmother holding the box that once contained the stir stick straws.

"Yes ma'am. You said I needed some product. What do you like to do and what's right in front of you?" I felt like a millionaire.

"Yes, I did say that…" My grandmother said, chuckling. "You sold straws?" Her deep and hearty laugh became fuller.

"Yes! I like drinking through straws and there was a whole big box of them in the basement right in front of me! You were right; it worked!" I started jumping up and down. "I can sell them all and have $100!"

"Naw chile, if these people bought straws this time, they won't buy them again. At least not right away," she said, shaking her head and laughing. "I can't believe they gave you money for these when I give them away for free." She went back into the living room and picked up the dollar bills from the floor. "You got $10 here. I'm impressed and proud of you. I am going to take $5 and give you $5."

"Why do you get $5?" I shouted, feeling cheated.

"Because you sold my product. Where do you think the straws came from? I had to buy them," she said.

"That's not fair," I said. My face had fallen. I looked down sheepishly at the floor.

"Life is not fair. But don't worry, I will find you some more product. Now run out and play."

I put my dollar bills into the envelope with the $10 I had received from my grandmother previously and stuffed it into the back pocket of my cutoff jean shorts. I went outside and headed down to the river that was just a few blocks from our home.

Sliding down the steep hill, my ashy big toes poked through the place where the rubber separated from the cloth on my muddy sneakers. I plopped down into the sand once I reached the river bank. I spread out my money—smoothing the bills out and placing them alongside each other. As the wind started to pick up, I gathered tiny piles of sand on top of each bill to keep them from flying away.

The waves dashed against the rocks. The cool wind blowing against my face felt refreshing and caused me to relax. My mind settled into processing through the day...

Twice my grandmother told me she was proud of me.

I could buy a lot of food with $15.

We rarely had food at my mom's house. Although she worked a lot, we didn't always have enough money for food.

To supplement our food supply, we went to a neighborhood food pantry once a month—as was our allowance, we'd steal food from stores, and, on the nights, we went to work with my mom, we got to eat food from the restaurants she worked in.

I had $15...I was rich! It was a satisfying day and I was content.

****

Each week for the remainder of the summer, my grandmother brought home boxes of candy bars, cases of soda pop, and bags of chips, and I sold all of it. For every case of product that I sold, she gave me $5. I forgot about poverty that summer, and my grandmother convinced me that if I worked hard enough, enjoyed my work, and gave people what they needed, that I could earn enough money to buy the things I needed to survive.

Chapter 2: Discovery

My mother, a petite, timid woman with wide teeth and a bright smile. Her skin was a smooth dark chocolate complexion and her high cheek bones and closely cropped, curly black hair made her beautiful. She and I were 16 years apart in age. My dad, the football hero that almost went pro, wasn't very tall. His strong, and fast frame complimented his clear and chiseled brown skin which made him an attractive high school star. My mother was on the school's dance team and they met when my father, who played for the visiting school, noticed her.

I was born the following fall and my grandmother helped to support us all until my parents got married, finished high school, and could afford an apartment of their own. My younger sister, Tanya was born when I was 4 years old, and by the time I was 6, my parents were divorced. My mother was so terrified that my father would find her after we moved out that she took extreme measures when dropping us off for visits with either him or his mom.

On the days we went to visit my grandmother (who was my father's mother) for the weekend or the summer, instead of waiting with us at the location my grandmother would pick us up from, my mother dropped my sister and I off at restaurants, stores, or at bus stops.

I always believed she just drove around the corner or was sitting across the street waiting with us secretly. When it was time to go back home to my mom's, my grandmother would drop us off in the same location she picked us up from, and she'd wait with us until she saw my mom pulling up nearby.

While we sat and waited to be picked up, I often daydreamed about what life was like for us. One of the last memories of my mom, dad, sister and me all living together was the Christmas before the divorce.

"We're going to have a big tree this year! I can see it," my father declared. On this day, he sat in his usual spot on our rent-to-own couch holding a big bottle of beer that he kept half wrapped in a paper bag to soak up the moisture from the bottle because then it was less slippery to hold.

At 24, his athletic features were softening behind his disappointed eyes and protruding stomach. He shaved every other day to avoid the bumps from ingrown hairs, and he shed his dirty khaki and black slacks and button up t-shirts for boxer shorts or pajama pants once he got home from splitting shifts between working at construction sites and his data entry job.

Even my grandmother knew that my father was quick tempered and had a drinking problem, but we tried our best to avoid his dysfunction and just not trigger him because he was juggling two jobs, a new family, and many responsibilities.

"We're getting a tree, daddy?" I shouted, jumping up and down with excitement in my red and black checkered, flannel pants and matching long-sleeved shirt. Unlike my grandmother, who required that I dressed like a girl at times, my parents let me pick out my own clothes. I could wear whatever I wanted.

"Yes, we're getting a tree and it's going to have lots of presents under it. You better be good, so Santa brings you lots of presents," my dad said.

With a furrowed brow, my father smiled through his words, took a swig of his beer, then rested his head back against the smooth, black leather. The Christmas before, we didn't have a tree and my parents couldn't afford to pretend Santa; we re-wrapped stuff from around the apartment and placed the items in the corner of the living room where we imagined a Christmas tree could be.

"I like presents and I will be very good, I promise," I said, smiling. I then collapsed dramatically onto the floor, sitting beside him, and hugging his feet.

"You're always good," my mother interjected. She was rolling around on the floor and playing with my 3-year-old sister, Tanya, whose slick, black curls cradled her chubby chocolate face. Tanya was wearing pink and purple wool, footed-pajamas that zipped up the front and had slippery bottoms on the feet. My mother was wearing a long white nightgown.

"Shut up Debra, nobody's talking to you," my dad snapped. He was irritated. My mother tended to cower inside herself, and my dad resented her weakness.

"Come on Sonny, let's just have a good night." My mother's teary eyes blinked incessantly as she smiled at my sister.

"Where is the tree going to go, daddy?" I asked, wanting to take my father's attention off my mother so that she stopped crying.

"I think it should go right over there in the corner; what do you think?" He motioned to the empty corner across the room.

"Let's put it in front of the big window!" my mother said. Her face lit up as she pointed at the large window that spanned the length of the living room of our apartment.

"How many times do I have to tell you to not speak if nobody is talking to you? It's time for bed, take the kids to the room, now!" my father shouted, slamming his beer down on the wooden end table.

My mother scooped up my sister from the floor, and I followed them to our bedroom. I pulled back the heavy cover and crawled into my twin bed as my mother tucked Tanya into the cozy cotton blankets of her matching twin bed.

Mother clasped her hands together and started the words, so that we mimicked her, to the bedtime prayer we always said together, "*Now I lay me down to sleep, I pray the Lord my soul to keep, and if I shall die before I wake, I pray the Lord my soul to take. God bless everyone in the whole world. Amen.*"

When it was time to turn off the lights, Tanya began to cry, so I climbed into bed with her and held her until she stopped crying and fell asleep.

My parent's room was on the other side of our room—we shared a wall. There was lots of moaning and grunting that night, and the incessant squeaking from the springs in their mattress distracted me from sleep so I laid there listening.

"Sonny, please stop," I suddenly heard my mother cry out! The sharp smack of leather on flesh followed, stinging the thick air between us.

"I will give you something to cry about," my father said.

He kept a long, black leather belt rolled up in the top drawer of the wooden chest next to their bed.

Whenever Tanya and I acted up, he'd tell us to get the belt and each time we stumbled out of their bedroom with it in hand crying in fear, he'd take the belt from us and shake it in front of our faces as he explained why he should use it. But he never did use it…at least not on Tanya and me.

My mother's cries and whimpering got louder and louder each time my father's belt snatched her skin that night and as he hit her, I covered Tanya's ears so that she didn't wake up from my or my mother's cries. On nights like this, my father's exhausted snoring was the cue that I could fall asleep, too.

While Tanya and I managed to escape his tirades, my mother was the punching bag my dad used to mourn his unrealized dreams.

"This is the second night in a row we are having pork chops," my father said one evening as we were preparing to eat around the quaint dinner table. His bloodshot eyes were tired and irritated.

"I'm sorry, they're leftovers from last night," mom said. "The bus was running late, and I didn't have time to stop at the store." My mom carefully positioned plates of meat and macaroni down on the table before each of us.

Each day after work, she'd catch the bus to my grandmother's to pick up Tanya, and on nicer days instead of getting back on the bus, she'd walk the few blocks to my bus stop where she waited for my school bus so that we all could walk home together.

After she got us settled in—Tanya with toys on the floor in front of the television and me seated at the kitchen table with my homework, she started dinner and other household chores so that all was ready when my father came home from work that evening.

"You could've told me to stop and get something. I am sick of eating this." My father squinted his eyes and scowled back in displeasure as he chewed a forkful of meat.

My mother sat down next to Tanya's high chair and scooped some macaroni and cheese into Tanya's mouth. "I'm sorry; I didn't think you'd mind," she said, intentionally avoiding his gaze.

"Oh, now you're thinking for me too?" My dad slammed his big fist on the plastic table covering making all our plates shake. I was so startled that I scooped a heaping spoonful of the orange noodles and a large bite from my pork chop into my mouth to save my food from falling onto the table if he were to strike again.

"No, I'm not trying to think for you, I just…"

My dad cut her off mid-sentence and yelled at me, "take your sister to the room. Now!"

Tanya and my mother both started to cry.

I anxiously pushed away from the table and pulled my little sister out of the plastic, yellow seat of her metal framed high chair and took her to our bedroom. Once inside, I decided to keep the door ajar and placed Tanya on a blanket next to a pile of toys. The brightly painted, wooden alphabet blocks, stuffed dolls, and happy meal toys distracted my sister's tears while my heart raced, and my mouth still tasted the creamy macaroni.

As my wide eyes peeked through the inches between the bedroom door and its frame, I saw my mother sitting in a folding chair across from the couch. She was crying. My father paced back and forth around the room. Each time he was in close proximity to her, he'd get in her face and threaten her, "I'm going to hit you."

He did this a few times before he walked to the coat closet and retrieved his metal baseball bat.

The same baseball bat he beat a mouse to death with once after he found it running loose in the living room. With the bat in hand, he towered over her chair and shook the bat in the air. "Don't make me do it," he yelled.

"I'm sorry, Sonny," my mother whimpered. "I promise I won't do it again…"

"Don't turn around," he shouted, as he walked behind her chair.

He swung the bat into the air and hit my mother in the back of the head, knocking her off the chair and onto the floor. He stood kicking her and yelling, "get up, you stupid bitch!"

Stumbling to stand, my mother sobbed quietly and covered her face with her hands.

"Shut the fuck up; it didn't hurt that bad!" my father yelled as he grabbed my mother by her waist and pulled her up to her feet.

He stripped off both their clothes as they slowly made their way down the narrow hallway toward their bedroom. When they walked passed our door, my eyes fixated in horror at the bright, red blood that was dripping from my mother's hair.

****

The first year after my parent's separation was unstable. We bounced around from place to place as my mom searched for a second job and a new apartment; and we slept in cars, on floor pallets in spare bedrooms, on the couches of the men my mom would find to give her money in exchange for sex, and in the booths of the fast food restaurants where my mom worked.

For a few days at a time, a family would host us in their home or apartment so that we had playmates while our parents were away working one of their many part-time jobs. Being poor was hard; kids aren't often supervised and must find ways to meet their own needs as parents work long hours at low-wage jobs.

We made floor pallets to sleep on in one of the bedrooms and during the days, I split my time between playing house with the other kids who were around and watching television. While we played house, we pretended that the littlest kids were our children, and those of us who were school age pretended to be the adults.

Sometimes my mom returned in a day or two, and sometimes she was gone for several days at a time and returned with things like pop, cereal, milk, lunch meat, bread, toilet paper and soap. When no actual adult was present, the older kids would take turns rotating house duty to stay inside with the littlest kids who couldn't yet walk or take care of themselves while the rest of us played. During the times between grocery visits when there was no food, it was also the responsibility of the older kids to dumpster dive for food.

At age 7, and then 8, I was among the oldest of the kids, and while I was genuinely terrified of mice and creeping things, I enjoyed when it was my turn to sift through the trash bins—especially the bins at a nearby bakery where I was always able to find pastries and deli sandwiches. I brought back anything that was wrapped, not damaged, and that didn't have maggots. After a day of foraging, I'd present my findings to my pretend family and we prepared a meal from the items that were gathered.

In addition to food, we also found household items in the neighborhood trash bins. Once I found an iron with a frayed cord. I brought the iron back to the apartment where we were temporarily living following my parents' separation.

"Where did you get this from," my mom asked that night as she was heading back to the room where our belongings were camped out. She had just gotten in from a late-night shift at one of the fast-food restaurants where she worked and was eager to get out of her work clothes.

"I found it in the trash. It's really cool! What is it?" I said as I proudly hopped through the room wearing a long t-shirt and cotton shorts.

My uncombed hair was wild and gnarly, and while I did wash up each day, I only bathed when we stayed in places with a bathtub. In public bathrooms and at places without a bathtub, my mom, sister and I would take what mom called a "whore's bath" — we would use a wet washcloth to wash our face, our armpits, and our genitals.

"Come on now—you know what an iron is. Don't be stupid," she said, throwing an annoyed glance across the room. She put the iron on the floor next to our mound of clothes.

"How do you use an iron?" I asked her.

"Come here, follow me." My mother slipped on a t-shirt, took off her bra through her sleeve, flung the stretchy garment into the pile of clothes, and picked up the iron.

I followed her to the kitchen where she grabbed a knife from a drawer and cut off the remainder of the cord.

"What are you doing that for?" I asked.

"When it's hot, it will smooth the wrinkles out of our clothes. Lay the clothes down flat and slowly move the hot iron over the clothes and the wrinkles will come out. Since the cord is broken we have to warm it up on the stove instead of plugging it in. I cut the cord so that the cord doesn't burn up." She placed the iron flat onto the stove that wasn't turned on. "Now, don't touch this damn stove. You hear me?" she said.

"Yes," all the kids in the room replied in unison.

"If you're not tall enough to use the stove, you can't use the iron,"
my mom said as her glazed eyes shimmered, reminding me of sleep.

****

"Where are we?" I asked sleepily as my eyes startled awake. The car
had come to a sudden stop and it was the middle of the night. My
mom had just gotten off work and we were all tired. This was one of
the nights my mom was unable to find childcare, so we colored,
played and slept in the booth of the restaurant while she finished her
shift.

"This is our new home," my mother replied as she motioned to the
tall, brick building behind her. She hopped out of the car, opened the
trunk, and started unloading the black garbage bags filled with our
belongings onto the dark street.

I took several moments to register her words and tried to look
through the night to see my new neighborhood. I saw a swing set
across the street, "Oh mom, can we play over there?" I asked
excitedly.

"Not tonight," she said. She hiked one bag over her shoulder and picked up another bag and handed it to me. "Maybe in the morning."

We walked up the skinny, wooden stairway attached to the back of the brick building and entered a darkened kitchen.

"Mom can we turn on the lights? It's dark in here," I said. Forgetting about the garbage bag I had been dragging, I grabbed my sister's hand because we were both still afraid of the dark.

"We don't have lights yet sweet thang!" Suddenly, a high-pitched voice emerged from the dark. My eyes focused to see a man standing there.

"Who are you?" I interrogated.

"I'm Slick, baby, but you can call me, Papa Slick," the man said. His smile was as bright as his skin. He was a thin, short man with curly brown hair. His pale skin smelled more rugged than it was.

"Y'all wait here, I got some candles in the backroom. Don't be scared; I'll be right back." Slick disappeared, and I could hear him whistling as his feet shuffled across the hardwood floor into the shadows.

"Mom, how long will we be here?" I looked up and saw her teeth smiling so I figured Slick was just another one of her tricks.

"Hopefully for a long time." Her voice was low and confident.

Slick came back with lit candles in hand and the light revealed his devilish grin. "Here, y'all take these," he said, "I got some more set up in the room back there for ya."

My mother and I each grabbed a candle, Slick picked up our garbage bags, and we all walked toward the backroom. Holding Tanya's hand and leading her along, I wondered how her 4-year-old mind was processing it all.

"Come on y'all, let's get ready for bed. It's late," my mother said as she motioned for us to come into the dimly lit room.

Slick placed the bags in the corner of the room and my mom began to undress—taking off her shoes then her pants. As she retrieved her pants from the floor to fold them, I saw her shadow outlined on the wall.

"Mom, your stomach on the wall is really round!" I declared, pointing to the shadow. Tanya's sleepy eyes followed.

My mom and Slick began laughing heartily. "That's because there's a baby in there! Now come on and lay down, your momma's tired," she said.

"There's a baby in there?" I asked, confused.

"Yes, there is, sweet thang," Slick said as he handed us each a pillow.

"How did it get in there?" I asked as I crawled onto the floor pallet and snuggled up to my mother who was holding Tanya in the crook of her arm.

"I put it in there," Slick whispered into my ear as he inched up close behind me.

"Now shush, let's get some sleep," he said, just before throwing an arm on top of me that extended toward my mother. That night, he rested his head on my pillow. I fell asleep underneath his heavy arm, listening to all our breath, afraid for what might happen next.

Chapter 3: Eternity

"Welcome home doll," Slick said, smiling as my mom and I unloaded the garbage bags filled with our summer clothes and toys from the car. "You have fun at your grandma's?"

"Yes, I had a great time. I got to work and make lots of money!" As I bounced onto the driveway, I eagerly retrieved the crumpled white envelope from my pocket to show my mom and Slick all the money I had made over the summer working for my grandmother.

"Let me see what you got there." Slick took the envelope and thumbed through the cash. "You easily have a hundred bucks in here." His eyes squinted, and his lips pursed.

"Let me see that!" My mom snatched the envelope from Slick.

"Now, Debra, you don't take things from me. Ok?" Slick was smiling at my mom as he took the envelope back from her. "Teasha, why don't you take your sisters inside to your room and unpack your things as we get ready for dinner," Slick instructed.

"Can I have my money back?" I asked, reaching my hand out to Slick for my envelope and for my new baby sister, Rose, who he was cradling in his arms.

"We are going to use this money to buy y'all some school supplies and some new clothes," he said.

At once, Slick handed me my new little sister, stuffed the envelope into his back pocket and called my mother inside after him. I took my sisters and headed to our bedroom as instructed, feeling completely deflated as I walked away from all the money I'd earned that summer. How would I guarantee that my sisters and I wouldn't run out of food the next time we are left alone for days at a time if I had no money?

****

"We're going to a party!" Slick shouted confidently as he shook me awake.

Our tiny bedroom was separated from the living room by a thin white sheet that hung in the doorframe. It felt more like a large closet or a home office than a bedroom, but it was warm, and it was home.

Our beds were red foam mats with one pillow for each of us and a blanket that covered all of us. My baby sister slept between Tanya and me. There was a stack of toys and board games hovering in the corner of the room and next to it was a mountain of garbage bags that contained our clothes.

"What kind of party?" I asked inquisitively.

"A birthday party! And it will be a lot of fun," Slick said as he snuggled on the mat between us.

I rubbed my eyes awake and asked, "Who's birthday party?"

"You ask a lot of questions, doll. It's your cousin's birthday. And I want you to look real nice too, so we're going to go shopping to get you something special," Slick said.

Slick's undershirts were always pressed and tucked neatly into his creased slacks, and he never buttoned his over-shirts all the way down. Even when just walking around the house, wearing shined shoes and all, he always looked as if he was going someplace important. And that made us feel important.

"I want to look nice like you," I said. "When are we going shopping?" I leapt from bed with excitement, startling my sisters who were already awake.

After breakfast, Slick took my sisters and me to the thrift store and my mother stayed at home. We looked at several racks of clothes. While my sisters crawled through the toy aisle, I pulled out several pairs of slacks and shorts and collected them into a pile in the shopping cart.

As I thumbed through the vests and long sleeve button-up shirts, Slick held up a sleeveless blue dress with a pleated bottom and asked, "How about this?"

"I don't want to wear that," I insisted, returning my gaze to the clothing rack. I was disgusted at the thought of wearing a dress because dresses are for girls and I'm not a girl.

"Oh, come on. I bet you'd be pretty in this dress. Try it on for me," Slick said in a whiney tone. He slid the dress between me and the hangers in front of me, and then rested his other hand on my shoulder. "Try it on for me," he whispered into my ear.

"Try it on? Where?" I felt like I at least owed it to him to try it on since he was begging.

"Right here. Try it on now."

I turned toward him, took off my dusty shoes, stepped out of my frayed jean shorts, threw my oversized t-shirt over the clothing rack behind me, and stood there exposed with my eyes closed feeling ashamed of my body as I wiggled into the dress.

"You look very nice," he said.

Slick lifted my chin and met my eyes as I opened them. I couldn't bear the thought of looking into the mirror at myself, so I took Slick at his word and trusted that I looked nice, enough. I took a deep breath then twirled around in a circle with my arms down at my sides.

Slick smiled—showing me his teeth. I smiled too. Rose and Tanya had dragged a few toys over from the adjacent aisle and played unaware. Slick then took my hands and we twirled together, laughing for quite some time.

After we paid for the dress, we returned home where my mother was there getting ready for work.

"Mom, look what I got!" I shouted, as I ran inside and threw open the plastic bag to show her my new dress. "Slick says I look nice."

I was just as excited about impressing Slick as I was excited for the birthday party because on the way home from the thrift store, Slick said there would be cake and ice cream. Cake and ice cream were treats we only ever enjoyed on special occasions.

"Call me Papa Slick, dear, ok?" he said, still smiling as he stood in the doorway.

"Papa Slick says I look nice," I said, correcting myself. I then took the dress out of the bag and held it up for everyone to see.

"Oh, that's nice..." my mom said. She was buttoning up her work uniform and not looking at me.

"Go get washed up and put on your new dress," Slick instructed as he sat down on the couch.

He was still holding Rose, who just recently learned to crawl. As I ran to the bathroom, I overheard them talking.

"You never buy me anything special," my mom said. Her voice, barely audible, quivered from the living room just a few feet away.

"Don't make this about you, Debra. And please don't ever question anything I do, ever again. Do you understand?" he said, in the kind of tone that ended discussions.

"Yes, I understand," my mother replied.

I returned from the bathroom twirling in my new dress, "I decided to call this my party dress! I can wear it to parties," I proclaimed.

Slick let out a roaring laugh.

My mother smiled and kissed each of us, silently, on top of our heads before disappearing out of the front door to work the night shift.

We walked down the alley to Slick's brother's house for the birthday party that evening.

Soon after we arrived, Slick disappeared into the kitchen with the rest of the adults—leaving us kids in the dining room where there was a host of games, treats, and the television to keep us occupied. The littler kids played with the white baby dolls and plastic Happy Meal toys that were strewn about the brown carpeted room while the older kids ran through the tiny bungalow playing tag and hide-n-seek. I sat on my knees in front of the floor model TV overwhelmed by so many people and so much noise.

"Why aren't you playing with the rest of the kids?" Slick asked, as he sat down on the floor beside me.

"I don't know," I replied. Just then, I lifted my knees and sat in a tucked position, burying my head in my lap.

"What's the matter?" Slick's voice became concerned and he began stroking my back tenderly. "What's the matter doll?" he asked.

"These kids are loud, and I want to go home," I lamented, as I began fidgeting with the hem of my party dress.

"You can sit here as long as you want. You don't have to play with them. You want to play with me?" Slick asked.

"I don't know." I shrugged my shoulders and lifted my head to rest it in the crook of his arm. The noise of the other kids faded away and I felt at ease as we sat for several minutes and watched an episode of Alf—one of my favorite TV shows.

"Let Papa Slick make you feel better," Slick whispered, as his soft stroking moved from my back to the outside of my thigh.

His hand then found its way underneath my dress into my underwear. At first, the tracing of his fingers tingled much like the tingling I felt after my baptism when I laid under the pew. But then the tingling sensation stopped, and I felt piercing pressure as Slick pushed his fingers inside me. The last thing I remember about the party that night was a deep and intense pain. Then I blacked out.

****

I awoke once during the night to Slick offering me a bowl of ice cream and cake, and I don't recall whether I ate any of it. The lower half of my body was sore and all I wanted to do was sleep and see my mom.

The next morning, I heard my mother rustling through the front door as she was returning from her overnight shift at the fast-food restaurant. I slid quietly out of the bed with my sisters and made my way into the living room.

"Mom, can I talk to you?" I whispered loudly across the room as her gaze met mine. She was shuffling through mail and Slick was asleep on the coach just a few feet from her.

"Talk to me about what chile? I just got off work and I'm tired." My mom kicked off her shoes and made her way into the kitchen.

I followed her. "I want to talk to you about the party," I said.

"Can't this wait until later?" She released a heavy sigh and shifted her weight on her feet.

"No mom. Please, can I talk to you now?" I started to shake.

"Have a seat," my mom said, pulling one of the metal chairs away from the rickety table. She motioned for me to sit down as she stood beside me. "What?" she said. She was impatient and afraid.

"Mom something happened at the party that I didn't like," I said.

"What do you mean something happened at the party?" She was peering down at me.

"Something not good." I was afraid to tell her what Slick had done because I wasn't sure what he'd do next. My shaking intensified as I remembered the pain from the night before.

"What happened?" she yelled.

"Mom, please be quiet," I whispered, as I began to tell her about the night. "Papa Slick touched me inside my underwear...and—"

She interrupted me and asked, "What do you mean?"

"He was rubbing my back at first and then—" Just as I was speaking, my mom slapped me across the face and I fell out of the chair and onto the floor.

"Why are you doing this? Your dad and your granny put you up to this, didn't they?" Her eyes were wide with fear as she stood over me yelling.

"No one put me up to anything," I cried, tears burning down my cheeks.

I held my face in my hands and scooted backward across the linoleum kitchen floor to get away from her.

"You're a liar and you're just like your father," she yelled, rushing toward me. "You don't want anything good for me." She grabbed me. "You want to take away everything don't you?" She started shaking me like a ragdoll.

"No, I don't want to take away anything," I cried. She slapped me again.

"Get up," she shouted, as she pulled me to my feet. "He never buys me anything special and he buys you a dress?" She punched me in the face and I fell back onto the floor. "You probably let him fuck you." She screamed, while hitting and kicking me.

I didn't hear my own cries. I imagined a giant, dark hole and I crawled into it.

"Debra calm down!" Slick yelled, as the light began to reappear in the room. I assumed he was the one who made her stop beating me as I laid there on the kitchen floor.

"You're protecting this bitch now?" my mom said, lunging at me again. This time, before she could hit me, Slick stepped in front of her and slapped her to the ground.

"You jealous, crazy bitch. I said calm down," Slick shouted. He then scooped me up from the floor and carried me into the bathroom where he cleaned the blood from my face.

My mother and little sisters were sobbing on the kitchen floor, and suddenly, Slick's haunting voice broke through their cries as he began to sing:

> One of these ol mornings, it won't be very long,
> You'll look for me, and I'll be gone...
> I'm gonna walk around heaven all day...

"You know, I love you. I love you more than I love your mom. I hate how she hurts you," Slick said as he brushed my cheek with a warm, damp cloth.

"I love you too..." I replied. I was cradled on his lap as we sat on the edge of the bathtub with my eyes as wide as they could open.

I was afraid to look at him because I didn't want him to hit me like he had hit my mother if I said the wrong thing, but I was more afraid to not look at him because his steady gaze kept the room from spinning. This was one of the first times anyone had ever told me they loved me that I could remember.

"Your mom hates you because you look like your dad. But I know that you can't help that. I think you're pretty," he said.

"You do?" My tears and my breathing slowed down. I felt less like I was going to vomit.

"Yes, I do," he said sweetly. Your skin is black, and your hair is nappy but you're pretty to me. Prettier than your mom." I focused on his words so that I didn't have to feel my body. "If you want, I can kill her for you. But then you'd have to marry me," he said. Slick chuckled to himself as he dipped the rag into the water in the sink.

"I don't want my mom to be dead," I cried. The tears welled up in my eyes again.

"She will keep beating you because she knows how much I care about you," he insisted.

"I don't want my mom to die," I said, terrified that he'd kill my mother.

Slick kissed the tears on my face and then whispered in my ear, "I'll never hurt your mom or your sisters again if you marry me. You could give yourself to me and we could run away to someplace where no one would ever find us."

"I don't want to run away," I pulled away from him. "I'd miss my daddy and my sisters and my grandma and my cousins." I felt like I was in a bad dream.

"Maybe you are as dumb as your mom." Slick put me on the floor and got up from the edge of the tub, throwing the bloody rag into the sink.

After he left later that day, he started spending less and less time with me. He took my sisters on special trips without me, leaving me alone with my mom, and when he crawled into bed with us at night, he didn't fall asleep snuggled next to me as often as he did before.

****

One Saturday afternoon, I was sitting on the floor in the living room playing with my toys when there was a knock on the door. Slick and my sisters were gone someplace, and it was just my mother and me.

"Good afternoon, are you Debra?" A cheerful white couple was standing outside of our apartment when my mom opened the chained door.

"Yes, I'm Debra. Who sent you?" she asked.

Mother never liked unannounced visitors, especially white ones. She always said, "white people who come over unannounced bring trouble."

"Well, it's Christmastime and we know you have some little ones and we wanted to bless you with some gifts to put under the tree." The man lifted a big paper bag and shoved it against the door smiling. His nose was red, and his skin was as bright as Slick's skin.

"Are you from the kids' school? Who sent you here?" she asked.

I panicked at the thought of those people being from my school. I went to school sometimes, but not very often.

"We hope you're not offended, we want to spread a little holiday cheer," the man said. Just then he peeked around my mother and looked into our living room. His eyes caught mine.

My mother slipped off the chain on the door and said, "Thanks for stopping by." She then took the bag of gifts and closed the door, tossing the bag to the floor in front of me.

"Are these for me? Can I play with them?" I asked, excitedly. I reached into the bag and began pulling out the toys. White dolls, board games, and action figures—toys I'd seen advertised but toys we'd never be able to afford.

"Come into the kitchen, I need to do your hair."

My mom left the toys in the living room scattered with me on the floor and set up her station next to the stove as she always did when she pressed my hair. She laid out the brush, comb, hair grease, and rubber bands on the counter and turned on the stove. I climbed into the rickety chair as she reached into the drawer to retrieve the metal straightening comb before placing it into the fire.

"Did you know those people?" she asked.

"No ma'am, I didn't." I replied.

She tilted my head down and her heavy hands began rubbing grease around my hairline. The smell of burned hair melted through the air as the comb was heating on the stove.

"Then how did they get my address?" Her voice was calm and low.

"I don't know," I said.

She parted lines down my hair hard with a plastic comb and smoothed more grease onto my scalp. I tried to remain calm, but I was terrified.

She grabbed the straightening comb from the fire and pressed it gently through a section of my kinky hair until it became straight. "I'll ask you again," she said, as she began straightening another section of hair. "How did they get my address?"

I hesitated to answer because I knew she wasn't looking for the answer I had to give. So, I remained quiet and tried not to move.

The narrow kitchen in our apartment was big enough for a card table and 4 chairs that sat underneath a window. My mother wasn't much of a decorator so there were no placemats on the table or pictures on the walls like there was at my grandmother's house.

The few dishes that we had were always stacked neatly in the cupboards. As I sat in the chair next to the stove, feeling the hint of heat on the back of my neck from the straightening comb, I wondered how long it would be before Slick came home with my sisters. I wondered if my grandmother was with her friends at church. It had been several months since I had visited her, and I wondered if she missed me. I thought of my dad and the nights I laid awake listening to my mother crying because of him beating her, and me feeling sorry for her.

"Don't sit there stuck on stupid now! You brought those white people to my house," my mother shouted as she began hitting me in the head with the hot straightening comb.

Heat from the comb and the weight of the metal knocked me off the chair and onto the floor.

As I laid in a fetal position, I covered my head with my hands. The tears didn't come because I learned that the more I screamed when she beat me, the angrier she'd become and the longer the beatings would last.

"You're just like your dad!" she screamed, "You want my life to be miserable! Why can't I ever be happy?"

After she tired from beating me with the hot comb, she turned off the stove, went into the living room, and lit up a cigarette. I laid on the floor and smelled her cigarette smoke until I was able to crawl back into the giant black hole that I created with my mind.

"What did you do, Debra?"

I heard Slick yelling and I opened my eyes to him standing over me and shaking me awake in the kitchen.

"That little bitch has it out for me. She brought the school to my house," my mother said.

"The school came here?" Slick's face was close to mine, but he was blurry.

"Yes, those fuckers brought Christmas presents to my house like I can't do for my kids," my mother shouted from the living room.

"You let them in?" Slick asked. Suddenly, he released me back onto the floor, and went into the living room. "You let those people in here, Debra?"

"No, I just opened the door. I didn't let them in," I heard my mother say.

I remembered the man standing at the door with his red nose.

"But you took the toys?" Slick inquired.

I wondered if Tanya and Rose had seen the toys on the floor in the living room.

"Yes, but they didn't stay. I just took the bag and they left."

"You are stupid, aren't you?"

Just then, I heard a loud thud and my mother screamed. I picked myself up off the floor and dragged myself to the living room. My mother was laying on the floor and Slick was squatting over her with his hands around her neck, squeezing.

I panicked. As much as she hurt me, I didn't want my mom to die. I went back into the kitchen and grabbed a knife out of the drawer. "Stop!" I yelled and ran toward them. Slick turned around and just as he stood up, the blade I was carrying met his thigh.

"I've done nothing but love you and now you hurt me like this?" he said. Slick hit the knife to the ground and chased me into the kitchen.

Still weak from my mother's beating, I knew I couldn't outrun him, so I stopped and turned toward him, "If you're going to kill me, do it now," I cried.

Slick's hands squeezed around my 9-year-old neck, and the room became eerily quiet. There were no thoughts in my mind— everything was blank. Weight and time disappeared, and I felt no pain or physical sensations. I was dying.

Suddenly, my mother appeared behind Slick and swung a baseball bat in the air, hitting Slick so hard that he collapsed on top of me, sending us both crashing onto the linoleum floor.

She rolled Slick off me and yelled for me to get up. "You're going to be ok. Just get up," she said, as she reached into his back pocket and retrieved his wallet. "Get up and go get your clothes. You're going to your granny's," she said.

At once, I struggled onto my hands and knees and crawled to my bedroom where I furiously shoved clothes into a garbage bag. It had become second nature to pack my belongings like this because we moved frequently, and when it was time to go, we always needed to move quickly.

My mom disappeared across the hall with my sisters. I assumed she dropped them off at a temporary babysitter because she came back alone. She grabbed me and the garbage bag I was filling—my mind wasn't clear enough to know what I had packed. We ran out of the apartment building, immediately climbing into Slick's car. As we started down the road, Slick ran onto the street screaming after us.

"Don't turn around and say anything to him. Sit your ass still," she said, as we drove frantically down the snow-covered street.

As we slid onto the freeway, she rolled her window down and lit a cigarette. She took a puff then said, "You must think I'm a fool, don't you?"

She exhaled, blowing smoke out of her rolled-down window. I didn't dare look at her and sat still, like she instructed, in the worn leather bucket seat. My head rested against the cold passenger side window. The cool glass was relieving to the pressure banging inside my head.

"You can go ahead and judge me if you want to, but I will tell you one thing, that man is the best thing that has happened to us. We had nowhere to go before him. Besides, I had it worse than y'all growing up, so go ahead and tell people what you want to," my mother said.

"It ain't that damn bad," she continued, after taking another drag off her cigarette. "We have a roof over our head and he takes care of y'all. What man does for another man's kids? That's more than I had. No body took care of me—I took care of myself," she said.

She took long, deep puffs of her cigarette; and I tried to count all the light posts we passed along the way to stay awake.

The car pulled up near a bench at a bus stop, "Just wait here," mother said. "Your grandma's on her way to pick you up. And here, take this…"

She handed me the cash she had taken from Slick's wallet and the knife she kept in the glove box. I got out of the car with my garbage bag hiked over my shoulder and sat on top of it in the dark with my money and knife until my grandmother arrived.

Chapter 4: That First Time

"Where is your sister?" my grandma shouted, as she approached me on the bench.

I had been sitting there that night counting the cars that passed through the intersection, but I kept losing count. "Her and Rose are at the neighbor's house across the hall," I said. The black bag crinkled beneath me like glass as I pushed down against its now frozen plastic to brace myself.

"Who is Rose?" My grandmother's eyes were warm and concerned.

"She's my baby sister." I stood up from the bench and stretched my stiffened arms into the air.

"Where is your hat? It's cold out here! And why are you holding a knife?" She grabbed the knife from my hand and threw it onto the street. I shoved the cash into my jacket pocket.

"My mom gave it to me," I said, startled and starting to cry because of her shouting.

"You aren't even wearing pants. What the hell is wrong with Debra sending you out here like this? How long have you been sitting here?"

In a long t-shirt, a jacket, socks and boots, I shrugged my shoulders because I had no concept of time that evening—this was before cell phones and a decent watch is something that would've been sold or stolen had I ever owned one.

My grandmother scooped me into her arms and carried me and my garbage bag to her waiting car, the engine idling. I buried my face into the crook of her neck and consumed her warmth. I was grateful she wasn't parked too far away because I was cold, tired and scared.

"Why are you crying?" she said, "I'm not mad at you. I'm mad at your mom for sending you out here like this!" She walked quickly as the snow crunched beneath her feet.

"I'm crying because you're shouting at me and I'm crying because it hurts," I replied.

"What hurts?" She sat me down into the warm backseat.

"Everything. My whole body hurts," I said as I stretched across the seat. I lifted my long shirt to reveal my bruised and battered body and began to cry.

My grandmother turned on the lights and turned up the heat inside the car. "Who hurt you like this?" she said, with a look of dismay. She then climbed into the back seat with me to more closely inspect my body.

"My mom and Papa Slick did. Please don't make me go back there. I will do anything if you let me stay at your house forever," I cried. "I will work for you every day and you can keep the money."

Just then, I reached into my jacket pocket and gave her the cash that my mom had taken from Slick's wallet.

My grandmother took off her coat and draped it around me. She pulled me close into her arms, held me, and rocked me while I cried myself to sleep.

A few days later, we got word that my mom, my sisters, and Slick left town. Although my parents had divorced, and my mom was with Slick, we all lived in the same city and my mother's family had stayed loosely connected to my father's family.

One of my mother's sisters called my grandmother to tell her that she had loaned them money before they left for Slick's hometown in Louisiana. Before hanging up, my grandmother made my aunt promise to call us back if she found out where they were staying or if she got a phone number for them.

"I hate them!" I wept, as I overheard my grandmother on the phone. "I never want to see my mom or Papa Slick again. I hate them, granny," I said.

Hanging up the phone, she walked over to me, leaned her head down and pulled me into her bosom. She'd been cooking and working in the yard that day and smelled of vanilla extract and fresh cut flowers.

"There is good and evil within and around all of us," she whispered over my sobbing.

"And some of us are sophisticated enough to recognize our powers. You must always choose good and love. You must always use your powers for good and for love—you hear me? God is good, and God is love," she said, sternly. "Hate will kill you…it will eat you alive…but the love of God will set you free." She spoke tenderly and softly, rocking us both as I quietly cried.

The first few weeks with my grandmother were hard. Each night, I woke up crying and sometimes hyperventilating as my body remembered the nightmare that had been my life. During these episodes, my grandmother got up and held me still. She'd sing or hum to me as she dabbed the olive oil on her hands that she reserved for anointing, and after she rubbed her hands together and etched an oily cross on my forehead, she laid one hand on my forehead and one hand on my shoulder as she prayed for me.

Her gentle words and peaceful energy calmed me down and once my tears and shaking stopped, she'd rock me back to sleep.

My grandmother was confident my physical wounds would heal but she was concerned about my psychological and spiritual wounds because of the nightmares and my inability to sleep through the night. And while her religious traditions taught her to abhor dependence upon Western medicine, and to live by faith in God alone for healing and wholeness, she trusted her better judgment and scheduled weekly appointments for me to see a child psychologist. Granny and I also prayed daily using the anointing oil, and we attended church events several times a week. In addition to work, family events and school, this was our routine that first year.

It would be several months before we heard anything about my mom, my sisters, and Slick again. And it would be several more months after that before they'd run out of money and eventually move back to Minnesota.

****

"I want you to pay close attention, ok. And tell me if there's anything you'd like to do," my grandmother said as we filed into a basement classroom of our church one Saturday morning.

The large room was separated into two rooms when the pastor pulled out the wall divider like an accordion. On the side of the wall where we were, there was a large table in the center of the room that was surrounded by chairs.

"Welcome to all current and potential new members," the pastor began. "I'd like to tell you about the opportunities available at our church. But before I do, let me offer a word of prayer and thanksgiving to our gracious God."

As the pastor began to pray, I looked around and noticed that I was the only child in the room sitting next to big men wearing fine suits and beautiful women dressed elegantly in their Sunday best—even though it was Saturday and not Sunday. The sea of dark faces felt familiar and reassuring. I didn't attend church when I lived with my mother, and if it was during a time my mother didn't allow us to visit my grandmother, I could go weeks and sometimes months at a time not attending church.

It was good to be back at church again.

That day, I heard about the usher's guild, the junior and senior Sunday school boards, the choirs, the deacons and deaconesses, the trustees, the nursery attendants, and more. There were so many ways to serve the church and each position had its own set of meetings and its own training classes. When we left that day, I was unsure of which service opportunity I wanted to participate in, so I agreed to do each activity that I could try.

I went to school during the days, and when my grandmother returned from work, we headed to church. Each day, except Mondays, we went to church. I served on committees, helped set up for events, served food during the on-site feeding program, cleaned the church after gatherings, and attended weekly worship services.

Church was no longer the place where I played under the pews and drew on the bulletins. I got joy from participating and being included. When we prayed together and listened to the preacher, I felt the same kind of peace that I felt when I listened to my grandmother as she prayed and spoke to me while she rocked me to sleep at night.

One Sunday morning, as the preacher stood before us, his booming voice became softer as he grabbed the microphone and stepped off the stage.

"The doors of the church are now open," he said. "If you want to give your life to Jesus Christ, make your way down the aisle and take my hand."

The choir stood up and blessed the crowd with a soft melody as the preacher extended one hand up in the air while holding a microphone in the other hand.

"Tomorrow isn't promised to any of us," the preacher said, "Won't you come..."

Just then, several people began making their way down the center aisle to shake hands with the pastor. Once they shook hands, a deacon ushered them out of the sanctuary and into a smaller office that was adjacent to the sanctuary, where the deacon would then collect their contact information and record their intentions for giving their life to Christ and joining the church community.

Our predominantly Black church attracted all levels of people from many walks of life. The people walking down the aisle that Sunday included a family of five—a mom, a dad, and three kids. Two boys and a little girl. They embraced one another as they made their way down the aisle and to the pastor and deacons waiting to receive them.

They reminded me of myself, my mom, Slick and my sisters. But they were a family that seemed to love God and one another; and they wanted to give their lives to Jesus Christ. I wondered what my home-life would've been like if my family all wanted to give our lives to Jesus.

Suddenly, the lights appeared brighter than usual. The pastor's voice on the microphone, more powerful than ever before. I didn't have words to explain it at the time, but I became captivated by the sacred energy swirling around the room. This was a holy encounter…an encounter with God. People coming one after another in response to an invitation that promised them everlasting life with God. I wanted in.

"If you've already given your life to Christ, and you've already been baptized, but you've fallen away, this is also your opportunity," our pastor said. "Rededicate your life to the Lord. God knows your heart and he knows your pain. Let him guide you back on the right path. Won't you come…"

The choir swayed together as a few more people made their way down the aisle to meet the preacher's extended hand. Something began to leap inside of me. Seeing the two dozen or so folks walk down that aisle was emotionally moving. Their eyes bright; their faces filled with hope. That made me hope.

Just then, the preacher started walking around the front of the room. He made his way back and forth down the aisle as he sang along with the choir. The congregation stood up, clapped and swayed to the gospel hymn. The movement and energy overwhelmed me, and tears flooded my eyes. My grandmother, standing next to me, was also swaying and singing along. I felt a fire rise within me and all I wanted to do was run.

So, I did.

I jumped up out of my seat and climbed past the people down our row. When I reached the end of the row, that fire propelled me from within and I bolted. I ran past the preacher and threw my 10-year-old body onto the steps of the altar.

I laid there crying out, completely unaware of the people packed neatly into the room. I ached on the inside and I wanted Jesus to take the pain away. That's all I could think about was Jesus; and somehow, I found him at the altar. I gave my life to him in that moment, and the more I cried, the lighter I felt inside.

Several other people from the congregation also began making their way to the altar at the front of the church. Some stood and bowed their heads in prayer, and some laid down on the floor beside me and began weeping themselves. Looking at the faces of the people through my tears and hearing their moans above the choir's soothing tunes made me realize that I wasn't the only one who had been hurt. The pastor made his way back up to the altar and prayed through the crowd, laying hands on all of us who were gathered there.

"Send your power and anointing to your people, O God, you know the pains of your people!" the preacher cried out.

When he got to me, he shouted, "God sees your pain. I speak healing over you in the name of Jesus." His thick hand rested upon my forehead and its warmth reassured me of God's love and power.

As he moved through the rest of the crowd, I studied the faces around me and for the first time in my life, I saw the Spirit moving. People with tears streaming down their faces. Grown men shouting at the top of their lungs in praise. Women running down the aisles yelling, "Thank you!" And each one looking more and more relieved as time passed.

As the pastor's prayer concluded and people started to return to their seats, I surprised myself and whispered, "I'm yours God, please take me."

When I returned to my seat, my grandmother leaned over and said to me, "The Lord is working on you, baby, and he's got you. He will never let you go."

I didn't fully understand all of what she meant but from what I had just experienced and from what she said, I knew that the power and energy I felt was much bigger than myself and stronger than any pain I could ever encounter.

Before that day, church was just a place I went to serve, listen to the preacher, and hang out with my grandmother's friends—it was never just for me. Sure, as Black people we went to church to escape the oppression of the world and to be reminded of our worth as human beings, but I had never considered the church to be a place for my own peace, until that day.

I felt closer to God than ever.

And God wasn't in the wafer that I broke apart into tiny pieces during my first communion all those years ago. God wasn't in the singing and swaying we did to the music each week. God wasn't in the tables I wiped or the bulletins I handed out before service. God wasn't even in the meals I served alongside my grandmother to the homeless people that filled our church's dining room every evening.

I left church that day more aware of the fact that everything we do as the church is out of a deeper knowing and awareness of God. God doesn't live in one specific place, nor is God constrained by the religious traditions we perform to experience closeness with God. God *is* the Energy that flows through us and every living thing.

"Granny, what happened to me on the altar today? Why couldn't I stop crying—I didn't feel sad…?" I asked, as I climbed into the backseat of my grandmother's car.

"You caught the Holy Spirit," she excitedly replied, before turning the key in the ignition.

"How did I catch the Holy Spirit?" My curiosity made me more than attentive.

"God is everywhere. But sometimes, if enough good energy—or what I like to call God-energy—is jumbled up in one place, you feel God so powerfully that you can't contain yourself. Some people sing, some people cry, some people dance, some people create—we all do different things when we catch the Spirit," my grandmother explained.

"How do we hold on to the Spirit once we catch it, so we don't lose it?" I asked. Still basking in the fiery peace I felt within, I couldn't stop smiling.

My grandmother began to laugh as she caught my toothy grin in the rearview mirror.

"Baby, you don't hold the Spirit, the Spirit holds you. You can't control when or how the Spirit moves, but you can nurture the good that's inside of you so that you're always able to recognize the Spirit when it comes."

****

Mr. Amen was our pastor. One afternoon, as I was helping to set up for the church's neighborhood feeding program, Mr. Amen came into the kitchen and asked my grandmother if he could take me out for a kid's meal and some ice cream. She welcomed the trip and he rejected the cash she tried to give him.

When we reached the church parking lot, I ran toward the car parked under the sign that read: *Pastor*. I stood near the rear of the car and waited for the pastor to catch up to me.

"Now, you sit up front with me," he said, as he walked past me to the front of the car. He opened the passenger side front door and held it open for me.

As I got in, I noticed how clean and shiny everything was. I had never been in a new car before.

"Wow, your car is brand new—hasn't anyone ever been in here before?" I said, excitedly. I ran my finger across the dashboard to check for dust like my grandmother did on cleaning day.

"No, it's not brand new, I just take care of it," he said. The smirk on his face was almost a smile.

"It sure looks new," I said. I sat back into the leather seat, inhaled the sweet smell of his car and closed my eyes.

"So, do you know why I wanted you to join me today?" Mr. Amen said.

"Because you want to take me to get something to eat."

I stared at him as he drove, studying his movements. His wide hands were wrapped around the steering wheel and the hair on his arms peeked out from the sleeves of his coat. His large frame relaxed against the buttery-smooth seat and his leather shoes tapped against the pedals. He was as clean as his car.

"That's part of it. But I also wanted to talk to you and get to know more about you," he said.

"What do you want to know, Mr. Amen?"

"For starters, why do you call me Mister Amen? Everyone else either calls me Reverend Port or Doctor Port. Well, not everyone else. My kids call me dad and Sister Port calls me James."

He laughed a full and hearty laugh. "So why do you call me Mister Amen?" he asked.

"Because every time you speak everyone says, Amen." I said, slightly surprised that he hadn't figured that out.

He erupted in laughter. "I think that's the best thing I've heard in all my life," he said. He laughed so hard he had to wipe tears from his face.

"What's so funny?" I inquired.

"I think it's adorable and you can always call me Mr. Amen. But I have to think of a nickname for you too, now."

"What will it be?" This prospect excited me.

"I'll think of it, and I'll let you know what I come up with."

We drove down the street to a burger place where he bought me a kid's meal and an ice cream cone as promised. Once our food arrived, we sat down in a booth to enjoy our meal. I ate the ice cream cone first. And as I wolfed it down, he began asking more questions.

"So, you've been living with your grandma for how long now—a year?"

"I guess it's been a year," I said, with a mouth full of the cool, creamy chocolate treat.

"How are you liking it there?" he asked, peeling open his burger container.

"It's much better than my mom's house but I do miss my sisters," I replied.

"Yes, I bet you do, but God will bring them home. We all will continue to pray." He took a bite of his burger and then placed it onto his napkin. "So how old are you?" he said, his mouth full now, too.

"I'm 10," I said.

The ice cream headache had set in, so I took a break from it and started to nibble on the crunchy cone.

"Yes, that's right. You're 10," Mr. Amen said. "And you've been really active in church a lot this past year for someone who is 10."

"Yes sir, I have."

"Does your grandma make you go to church?"

"She says everyone living under her roof has to go to church on Sundays, but I choose to go the other days."

"Why is that?" He took a couple more bites of his burger then took a swig of his soft drink.

"Because I like it," I responded. I was nearing the end of my ice cream cone and eager to see what toy was waiting inside my kid's meal.

"What do you like about coming to church on all those other days?"

"I like the people and the stuff we get to do and learn about."

"Do you like school too?" Mr. Amen unbuttoned his sleeves and rolled them back before diving into his French fries.

"Yes, I like the learning part, but I don't always like the other kids," I said.

"Oh no, why not?" His brow furrowed as he shoved more fries into his mouth.

"Sometimes they make fun of me," I said. Just then, I took a deep breath in and released it, trying to forget about the kids at school who made fun of me.

"What do they make fun of you for?" Mr. Amen said, with a puzzled look on his face.

"They say I look poor and that I'm slow because I don't know some stuff."

"Kids can be so cruel. I'm sorry they make fun of you. If you study really hard and go to college, you will grow up and find a really good job and you'll be able to dress and look any way you want to." His voice was kind and his gentle eyes made me believe him.

"I could even look like you?" I asked.

"Yes, I suppose so. I don't look half bad!" He chuckled and wiped his mouth with a napkin, then said, "What do you want to be when you grow up?"

Instead of using my napkin, I wiped my mouth with the back of my hand then wiped both hands on my jeans. "I want to be a minister or a doctor," I said, with a mouth full of the delicious cheeseburger I was enjoying. It was rare to have a kid's meal.

"Praise God! That's wonderful. And who knows, you might become both a minister and a doctor." Mr. Amen smiled wide.

"How can you be both?" I was puzzled.

"Well, I'm both a minister *and* a doctor," he said.

"You are?"

"Yes, but I'm not the kind of doctor you're thinking of. There is a doctor that works in a hospital and there are other doctors who work in other places, too. Doctor is the title you get when you have the highest college degree."

"You have the highest college degree?" I was impressed with him because no one in my family had a college degree.

"Not *the* highest degree—there are other folks who also have doctorate degrees. I'm special but not that special," he said, chuckling again. "You know what, I've got it! I've got a nickname for you."

"You do? What is it?" My eyes beamed with excitement and I forgot about my kid's meal toy.

"I'm going to call you, Little Amen," he said, with wide eyes and a big grin.

"Little Amen. I like that," I said, after pausing a few seconds to think it over.

After that day, when my grandmother and I went to church, Mr. Amen and I spent as much time as we could together. I helped him with odd jobs around the church, and we'd talk while we worked. He supported my enthusiasm for learning, and he convinced me that I should ignore the kids who made fun of me because he said I was smart enough to go to college someday.

Moving in with my grandmother was a difficult transition to make. Spending time with my grandmother and Mr. Amen, going to church and the child psychologist, and learning about God helped my wounds slowly begin to heal.

And although Mr. Amen moved to another church a short time later, I cherished our holy moments together. Through him I realized that the more I have to look forward to, the less I have time to think about the pain I went through.

Part 2. I Am in Transition

Chapter 5: From Death to Life

My confidence progressively expanded as I gained leadership and social skills at church. This propelled me through my childhood and adolescent years. I joined student leadership groups in school and played many sports. In middle school, I added gymnastics, modeling, math league and the debate team to my list of hobbies.

By high school, I was in the sign language club and was voted class president for three consecutive years. I participated in the school's Bible study group and was a certified peer mediator. I even helped to start an afterschool social group to promote tolerance and community advocacy for students, called GSA (gay straight alliance).

Ellen DeGeneres had recently come out as lesbian to the public in a Newsweek article, and as much as I had rejected that label for myself, I was aware that there were gay and lesbian students in my high school who might have felt marginalized. I wanted to connect with them and build greater awareness about the LGBTQ culture.

I logged many volunteer hours and was regularly invited to special events and award ceremonies. Each semester I was on the 'A' honor roll and when I wasn't in church for an event, I was at school because of an event. Every day was filled with something exciting.

At school, my friends were everyone—the jocks, the cool kids, the smart kids, the grunge kids and the queer kids. After school, a few days a week when I wasn't in church activities, I worked at the gas station to make money for clothes, sports, and activities fees. And that is where I met Sammie.

Sammie was a regular customer who came into the store and talked with me a lot while I worked. I couldn't tell if she was male or female at first, and this intrigued me. With short, curly black hair and a stocky frame that was covered by large shirts and oversized pants, it was easy to mistake Sammie for a boy until she spoke. After several months of her coming to the store and hanging out with me—sometimes more than once during the same shift, I asked her out on a date. She said, "yes" and for our first date, we caught the bus to the movies.

****

My grandmother was standing in the living room one evening as I had come home from work. "Are you a lesbian?" she asked me, as I turned the knob and opened the door.

"No, grandma I'm not a lesbian," I replied. I closed the door and tried to walk past her,

She then stepped in front of me with her hands folded across her chest, letting me know it was unwise to make any further movements.

"I thought it was a phase but then I saw you holding hands with that thing at the bus stop. Is that a boy or a girl?" she asked, her voice lowering. Her face was pensive, and her eyes were unkind.

"There is nothing wrong with holding anyone's hand and that *thing* is a person. Sammie is a girl," I shot back, defensively.

"A girl, huh...?" she said, beginning to pace the floor. She was becoming visibly upset; I had never seen her this way before. "What about Scot?" she snapped back, now with her hands on her hips.

I could no longer look at her in the eyes because I was immediately triggered to the time I lived with my mom and I feared my grandmother's growing anger and what the physical manifestation of that anger could become.

"What about Scot? We dated, and we broke up," I said.

"Was he a boy?" my grandmother asked.

"Yes, Scot is a boy," I replied smugly.

Scot is a boy who was in my youth group at church that I had a crush on since junior high school. Whenever we were at church together, we sat next to one another and after church events, we'd sit and talk until Scot's parents and my grandmother were ready to leave.

He lived in a different part of town, so we never went to the same school. After high school started, and I began hanging out with the kids from GSA, I realized that I needed to be honest with Scot about my attractions to people regardless of their gender identity.

"You need to pick a side," he said, as we were talking on the phone one Sunday evening after church. I told him about the support group and how I had also been attracted to girls, guys, and ambiguous people.

"I don't need to pick a side; I'm queer-identified," I proudly proclaimed to him.

"You do need to pick a side. Bisexuals are confused. You can't like boys and girls. And what is queer-identified? I once thought I was bisexual but now I know that I am not," he explained.

Scot was tall and dark. His acne and the fact that he hadn't yet grown into his nose gave away his age. I liked him because he believed in God and wasn't embarrassed to admit it.

That evening, I was laying on the floor in front of the TV in the living room. Wearing just a pair of boxer shorts, I winded up the telephone cord with my fingers and stared up at the ceiling as our post-pubescent conversation unfolded.

"Queer-identified is a term that covers a wide range of sexual identities," I replied.

"It's like bisexual, but it basically means I can just be whatever I am, and I don't need to pick a side. I read about it," I said. "How did you figure out that you're not bisexual?"

"I watched porn with my older brother and seeing the women turned me on so much that I had to jack off."

"Ok, that's gross—and that doesn't prove anything. You could've been turned on by the guys, too." I said, as I laughed into the phone.

"No, my brother says that women have this effect on men and that it is clear I ain't no sissy. You need to pick a side."

"Whatever Scot. You can't tell me what I need to do. Just because you picked a side doesn't mean I have to. I know several people at my school who don't feel the need to pick a side."

"What would your grandmother say about this?"

I yelled through the phone, "She will never know because she couldn't handle it. So, you're not going to tell her. Promise me you won't tell her Scot!"

"Calm down, I was only playing. I know how the elders at church get about anything sex related. You won't catch me talking about being bisexual with any of them. Besides, I don't want anyone thinking I'm a sissy."

"Stop saying sissy. I hate that word." I rolled my eyes as if he could see them through the phone.

"What else are they? My brother says sissies are like girls because no real man would ever want to be with another man."

"Your brother is a jerk."

"No, he just doesn't like faggots."

"I'm hanging up. You're an ass."

"Come on, come on. I'm sorry…"

"I have guy friends who are gay, and I don't want you talking about them like this. They are nice people and you're talking about them like they don't matter."

"I'm sorry."

"Ugh. I should go."

"No, come on, don't hang up. I'm sorry. I won't talk about your friends no more. Come on."

His begging through the phone was cute, so I forgave him and said, "Fine, but don't be such a jerk. Besides, you might still be bisexual and then you're gonna be the sissy!"

"Fuck you. I ain't no sissy," Scot interjected.

I succeeded at hurting his pride. "It hurts being called names, doesn't it?" I laughed.

"I'm not into guys and I can prove it!"

"Sure, you can…"

"Yes, I can!"

"How?" I wasn't convinced, and Scot knew it.

"Have sex with me?" he said.

"Excuse me?"

"We are boyfriend and girlfriend, and we love each other. And if you want to pick a side, it makes sense that you have sex so that you can know for sure."

"What would God think about us having sex? We aren't married." I was terrified at the thought of having sex with him.

"What would God think about you being bisexual? It's the same thing. You *can't* be this naïve."

"I'm not naïve, I just don't think we should have sex before we get married. My grandmother says that sex is reserved for married people."

"They only tell us that to scare us. Anyone can have sex."

"I don't want to catch anything. There are so many STDs. And AIDS, I don't want AIDS. And I sure as hell don't want to get pregnant."

"That's why there are condoms. You can't catch something from someone that doesn't have anything anyway. Say, sorry to change the subject, but you told me you needed that calculator for school, right? I think I got one for you."

"Really? Oh my God! How did you get one? My grandmother says we can't afford it this semester and by the time I'm done saving for it, the semester will be over. I cannot fail this class. I need this calculator. How did you get one?"

"I have a boy who can hook me up with one. He goes to another school and says he can get anything."

"Tell him to get me a graphing calculator and I will pay him anything."

"Ok, bet. I'm on it. Let me call him now."

"Ok, Scot. Thank you. I love you."

"I love you too."

I hung up the phone smiling and laid on the floor thinking about this calculator. Up to that point I had received A's in all my classes and the advanced math class I was in was the only threat to my grade point average because I couldn't afford the graphing calculator we needed to use.

A few minutes after I started daydreaming about my new calculator, the phone rang, and the caller ID revealed that it was Scot again.

"Hi Scot. What did you forget to tell me?" I asked, hoping he could hear my smiling through the phone.

"I didn't forget nothing, I just have some news."

"What's up?"

"I spoke to my boy and he can get the calculator this coming Tuesday. So that means I can come over and bring it to you Wednesday. Do you think you could skip school?"

"Oh, I don't know about that…"

"Come on, your grades are like perfect. No one is going to be mad because you miss a day. Besides, during the day on Wednesday is the only time I can bring over the calculator, unless you want to wait all the way until Sunday to get it at church. Shit, you don't even have to miss the whole day, just go in late on Wednesday."

"I don't want to wait all the way until Sunday when I could literally just have it in a couple of days. If I don't have to miss the whole day, I can just lie and tell the office I had an appointment. Are you sure you can get it? And are you sure you can get here early so that I can make it to school?"

"Yes, my boy has always come through for me."

"Ok, I should work on homework and get off the phone. Let's talk tomorrow. I am so excited to see you Wednesday morning. Tell your boy that I said, thank you."

That Wednesday morning, everyone left the house like usual. My grandmother went to work, and I got on the bus for school. When we arrived at school and everyone dispersed, I walked around the block, down the street, and to the city bus stop. I caught the bus back home and waited for Scot. Skipping school made me nervous and my heart was pounding through my chest the entire ride home, but I was excited to finally get a graphing calculator.

"Hey there! I'm glad you made it," Scot said when he arrived.

I closed the door, locked it, and made sure the curtains were pulled closed so that no one could see that I had skipped school and was inside. Scot was wearing his backpack and school uniform—brown khakis and a black polo shirt. He kicked off his white sneakers and tossed his backpack onto the couch.

"Yes, I almost missed the bus, but I caught it. Nice place. I figured it would be bigger though," he said while hugging me onto the couch.

"My grandma works very hard and I do too, but money doesn't stretch very far," I said, sitting up beside him. I was embarrassed.

"I'm sorry, I'm not trying to talk about your house. It's nice." He put his arm around me and pulled me close. "Hey, I got something for you. My boy came through."

Scot unzipped his backpack to reveal the calculator.

"Oh my God!" I squealed. "That's just like the ones they have at school. They're like $200. How much does he want for it?" I grabbed the calculator out of Scot's hand and slid off its grey cover.

"I took care of it, so you don't need to pay for it." He said, smiling.

"You'd do that for me?" I couldn't believe it; $200 was a lot of money for my family.

"I love you. Besides, I know a way you can pay me for it and you don't have to pay me a dime."

"You want me to have sex with you, don't you?" I asked, as I sat back on the plush, green couch.

"Yes! Don't you think it's time? We've known each other for years and we go to the same church. It would be great to lose my virginity to someone I know and trust. My brother had sex for the first time with a girl he didn't even know—and he had to pay her for it. Cash!" His voice sounded nervous.

"I don't want to get pregnant, Scot," I exclaimed.

"I brought a condom; my brother gave it to me." He retrieved the gold, foil-wrapped square package from his backpack and held it up to show me.

"I really need this calculator..." I said, feeling like I owed him.
"What do you want me to do?" I asked next.

"Just take off your clothes and lay back," he said.

Reluctantly, I did as he instructed. He bit off the corner of the foil wrapper, spit it to the floor, and then took off his pants and boxer shorts.

"What is that?" I screamed, jumping up from the couch.

"What is what?" he said, slightly startled. He then rolled the condom onto his penis.

My 16-year-old eyes immediately widened, "Your penis is huge!" I shouted.

"Is it too big?" He stood there facing me.

"I don't know. How big is it?" I couldn't take my eyes off it.

"When it's completely erect, it's almost 8 inches," he said. A look of panic covered his face.

"Jesus Christ. And you want to put that inside of me?"

"My brother says girls like big dicks. Just lay back!"

He guided me back onto the couch and braced himself onto one elbow while he slid between my thighs. I took a deep breath as he began to penetrate me. The pressure was unbearable. After the second thrust of his hips, my head started to swim, and the room started to go dark.

"Stop. I can't do this," I said, shaking my head so that the room could become clear again.

"What do you mean?" His body stiffened as he looked intently into my eyes.

"Scot, I can't do this. I haven't felt this way since I was a little kid, please stop." I began to cry.

Startled, Scot quickly got up and stood next to me and said, "Please don't cry, I'm sorry. What did I do wrong? Is it too big?"

"Scot, I'm sorry. You can keep the calculator, but I can't do this. It's not you…It's him." I started sobbing with my head in my hands.

"It's who?" Scot said, as he yanked off the condom and pulled on his clothes. He picked up my clothes from the floor and handed them to me. "Should I go?" he asked.

"Yes, Scot, I think you should go." I sat up on the couch and felt a stickiness between my legs.

"You can keep the calculator," he said, as he headed toward the door.

After Scot left, I took a shower to try and wash off the morning. It had been years since I thought of my youngest sister's father, Slick, but my body couldn't help but remember him in those moments with Scot. I sat down in the tub and let the water wash my tears and memories down the drain. Scot and I didn't talk much after that day, and he didn't come to church much anymore either.

****

"So, you broke up with Scot because you're a lesbian?" my grandmother said, interrupting my memories. Her brow furrowed with confusion, and she let out a deep and heavy sigh.

"No grandma, we broke up because we broke up. And I'm not a lesbian; I am attracted to the spirit of a person. I don't care what genitals they have," I tried to explain.

Over the years we had talked openly about everything except sex and my identity, but in this moment, I wanted her to understand me. Suddenly, she lunged at me and wrapped her hands around my throat and began to squeeze. Her eyes were filled with hatred and her face looked afraid—almost like she was looking into the face of a demon.

"What have I done to deserve this? I've always kept a job; my grades are excellent, and I've never been in any trouble. You always brag about me at church and now you're choking me?" I gasped for air between words and tears to maintain my breath.

"Yes, let's talk about church. What would God say about all this?" she said, loosening her grip around my neck.

"There is a difference between God and the church, and God wouldn't want you to choke me, I can tell you that much," I said into a puddle of tears on the floor.

My grandmother was my hero; she had taken me in when my parents were incapable of caring for me. She had introduced me to spirituality, helping me develop a love for learning and the church. Now, suddenly, she was treating me like a stranger she hated.

"Oh, now you're being smart!" she said, towering over me as I laid on the floor in a fetal position.

"I'm just answering your question. Can I go to my room please?" I felt the walls closing in and the room beginning to go dark. I had not dissociated mentally since grade school because I learned to control my anxiety through prayer, but this time the darkness was coming fast.

"I will not have that here. You carrying on like this all around town! I read your journal while you were out with that—that girl. I knew something was different about you when I first took you in—stuffing socks in your underwear and running around here like a little boy. I cannot have this under my roof."

"You read my journal? It's under my mattress? You went through my things?" I screamed back, feeling violated.

We recently moved into a 2-bedroom townhome and it was the first time, since before my parents' divorce when I was 6, that I had my own bed. Up to that point I'd slept on couches, in beds with others, or on floor pallets.

I'd seen on TV shows that people put their diaries and journals under their mattress. I was excited to now have a mattress to stash my journal under. That excitement quickly faded as my grandmother continued to berate me.

"Everything in this house belongs to me and I am putting my foot down," she said, sternly. "I know you had problems when you lived with your mom and I'm sorry about that, but she is sick and couldn't help that she hurt you guys or let you be hurt by that man. I raised you better than *this*, though," she said, shouting angrily and spitting while she spoke.

"Better than what? Better than loving people for who they are and not judging them like you're judging me right now? My mom has nothing to do with this, but since you want to bring her up, did you know she's also attracted to both men and women? She told me herself that she's had girlfriends and boyfriends," I shouted back.

"I don't know about any of that," she said, surprised, "but if you want to stay in this house and stay at the church, you will not be carrying on like this—like some sort of demon whore!"

"Why would you call me that? Seriously. I've never done anything to hurt you and I've always helped out in every way I could and now you're going through my things and calling me names and choking me?" My tears wouldn't stop. After all those years, I thought she was different than my mom, I thought she actually loved me.

But she was no different.

"I cannot have this in this house," she screamed. "If you want to be some hippy freak and love everybody, then do it somewhere else because God created Adam and Eve. He created woman to be with man; that's it! That's what the Bible teaches and that's what I believe!"

"That's what the Bible teaches? That's what church teaches about the Bible, but we pick and choose what we believe as truth. Did you know there are two different creation stories in the Bible and that they weren't written until after the book of Exodus was written? What about that? The Bible also says we shouldn't eat shell fish, do you want to choke me for liking shrimp? Next you're going to tell me that we should go back into slavery—because the Bible says that's ok!"

I immediately got up from the floor, pushed my grandma out of the way, and went into the bathroom that was directly behind her to get tissue to blow my nose that was now running.

"I've heard enough. If you want to go to hell, be my guest but I am not condoning this. You will not sleep here tonight!" she screamed.

I convinced my grandmother to let me pack my things and to give me a ride to my dad's house. Although I had not lived with my father for almost a decade, I knew that he couldn't turn me away and I couldn't think of anywhere else to go.

The 10-minute drive to my dad's house was spent listening to my grandmother tell me how evil I was and how she's always known I was different. I drowned out most of her words by reciting the 23rd Psalm in my head.

After I unloaded the garbage bags full of my belongings onto the grass, my grandmother drove off in her silver minivan, and didn't look back.

"Can I stay here with you, dad?" I shouted, as I knocked hard on the white aluminum door.

My dad opened the door to his 2-bedroom townhome that was scarcely decorated with a couch, a recliner, and a large glass coffee table with pictures of me and my sister, Tanya—pictures that had been taken years beforehand while my parents were still married.

"You are my firstborn, and nothing will ever change that. You can stay here," my dad said warmly.

My dad and I have almost identical facial features and hairline, and by that time, we were also the same height. Wearing a white t-shirt and zebra print pants, he smelled like beer and cigarettes, and it appeared he hadn't shaved for a few days. He helped me carry in my things and showed me to my new bedroom up the narrow staircase.

When we reached the top of the stairs and I entered the bedroom, he then said to me, "Granny called me this morning and told me what's going on. She said you're a dyke."

"Dad, please don't call me a dyke. And if I was a lesbian, so what?" I said, while unloading my garbage bag of clothes and knickknacks onto the twin bed.

"So, what? That's nasty," he said, standing in the doorway watching me unpack. "Being gay is nasty. It's hard enough to be black in this world and now you want to be black *and* gay? You're just asking for people to hate you. I can't believe you do…that!"

Just then, my father scrunched up his face with a look of complete disgust and he brought his hand up to his bloated stomach as if he would physically become sick.

"I didn't come here to have you think about me having sex, dad. The idea of you having sex completely grosses me out too but I still love you!"

"Ok smartass. I'm not thinking about you having sex, I just don't understand why you have to be gay."

"Being attracted to someone is not a choice. Besides, I don't have to have sex with anyone to know who I like."

I felt defeated and deflated, and I couldn't look him in the face because I was scared to see hatred in his eyes like I had seen in my grandmother's eyes.

"It's still nasty!" he barked, before turning to go down the stairs. "You can stay here and finish school if you'd like but don't bring it here; I don't want to see it or hear about it."

I slept there that night and stayed for almost a week. The constant barrage of comments about how disgusting he thought I was began to wear me thin and I decided that it was better to live on the street than to hear his demeaning and derogatory thoughts about me.

****

After leaving my father's house, I made my home inside myself and dwelled in many places around the city. I carried a blue and black backpack that contained a spiral notebook, several pens, my Bible, a change of clothes, a washcloth, toothpaste, a toothbrush and a bar of soap that was in a plastic Ziploc bag.

My books were in boxes at my grandma's and my clothes were in garbage bags at my dad's. I made stops at each residence a couple of times a week to retrieve books and to wash my clothes when I knew that no one would be home.

I worked the early morning shift at the gas station where I could wash up and then I went to my summer internship that I had at the hospital. When I left the hospital, I'd find a coffee shop, drop-in center or restaurant to sit at for a few hours and use payphones to call my younger sisters.

At night, I scattered my prayers and memories in ink while riding the city busses until my bus transfer ran out. Once my transfer ran out, I took long walks along the Mississippi River, I slept on the couches of friends whose family could spare a night or two, and sometimes I slept squatted in dimly-lit places that didn't have much traffic.

By the end of the summer, I was tired. Tired of roaming, tired of watching my back on the street, and tired of feeling alone.

I hadn't been to church in months and I missed my sisters. I was an outcast.

"Granny, can I talk to you?" I decided to call the house from a payphone one morning.

"What do you want?" Her voice was sharp and uncaring.

"I'd like to have a meeting with you and talk to you." I was desperate.

"You ain't in trouble, are you?"

"Granny, can we just have a conversation?"

"Come by after work today." Her tone suddenly changed, and she seemed more genuine.

"Yes ma'am," I said.

I hung up the phone and I started to pray. I didn't know what I would say to my grandmother, but I was hoping that God would give me the words to say and the courage to face her.

When I got there that afternoon, the house felt different but looked the same. My grandmother was in the kitchen sitting with her hands folded on the polished round table.

Still wearing her long, blue work coat and black slacks, she asked, "Is the Prodigal Son ready to come home?" The smirk on her face and patronizing glance made me instantly regret the decision to meet with her.

"I'm so close to graduation. I just want a steady place to sleep and do my homework. That's it," I said, speaking quickly. I hated that I needed her.

"I hope you learned a lesson out there. Cut out all this nonsense; you ain't a homosexual." She moved closer toward me and held my gaze.

"Yes ma'am," I said, lowering my head then repenting for the lie.

"You can stay here until graduation, but you can't be gay—don't bring it here. I don't want to hear nothing about it and you better not make any of the other kids gay."

"Yes ma'am." Emotionally, I began to sink deep within myself. I couldn't believe she was acting as if I was a complete stranger—like she didn't know my character or trust me at all.

"And don't be flaunting it around town where everybody can see you. I bet not see you at no more bus stops or anywhere with that man-woman." She was disgusted but for some reason there was a glimmer of hope in my grandmother's eyes.

"Yes ma'am," I replied. My stomach tightened, and I felt sick.

"I'm not comfortable with you at church because everyone will talk. You know who this family is for the community—I just don't want egg on my face."

"Yes ma'am." My tears started slowly.

"You can be here until you're done with school, then you gotta go. And you sleepin' on the living room couch where I can see you. So, there's no funny business."

"Yes ma'am," I said. I couldn't look at her.

"Go on now, get washed up. You look pitiful but that's what happens when you become enslaved by your sin. We are going to set you free today. Get washed up. My sisters are coming over and we're gonna pray this demon out of you.

"Yes ma'am."

I got up from the table and retreated to the bathroom with my backpack that still had in it a change of clothes along with my Bible, notebook and pens. I sat on the floor of the bathtub and cried for some time over the sound of the steaming shower.

I prayed for God to give me strength and when the hot water had left, I got dressed and decided to face the world waiting for me on the other side of the bathroom door. When I stepped out of the bathroom, I was met by my grandmother who instructed me to follow her into the living room. She moved quickly.

"Here she comes!" Whispers and chatter from the living room revealed 4 of my grandmother's sisters and several women from the church.

These women, large in every sense of the word, were standing together in a circle. They were the matriarchs and whenever anyone talked about them, they were simply referred to as "the Aunties" because these powerful, Black women moved as a unit and looked and lived similarly to one another.

They were devout Christian women who raised an army of children between them while holding notable positions in the church and community despite the daily realities of sexism and racism. Every child in their presence became their child—and we all knew it.

"Come stand in the center," an aunty said.

My grandmother and I made our way through the formation to stand in the circle. I scanned the room and noticed that where the coffee table had been was now an open space, the curtains were drawn shut, and the couch had been pulled out of the way and into the kitchen. I felt like I was entering a den of lions and somehow, I knew no miracle would keep them from devouring me.

Another aunt approached me and laid her heavy brown hand on my forehead and began to pray. Soon after, each of the Aunties and my grandmother extended their hands toward us. I was afraid to close my eyes. The first aunt began praying so loud that it was as if she was screaming and she began speaking in a language I had never heard before. They all began to wail and moan.

After several minutes of this, the aunt who had her hand on my forehead opened her eyes and looked into mine.

"The devil is strong in this one," she exclaimed! "Look at her standing here with her eyes completely opened—unmoved and confident."

My grandmother stepped forward, holding her bottle of olive oil that she used for anointing during prayer. She dipped her finger into the bottle and then rubbed it into the shape of a cross on my forehead. The first aunt began to pray again, and the other dozen or so Aunties joined in. Each put a hand on my head, or as close as they could get, praying, murmuring, and wailing for several minutes. I was too stunned to close my eyes.

"Satan, I bind you in the name of Jesus and I command you to come out of this child," an aunt screamed into my face! The spit and sweat dripping from her lips made my stomach turn. My heart was racing.

"The Lord is working on her, look at her," another aunt yelled! "We gonna get this demon out! Satan you loose this chile!"

The first aunt began to shake me, and the others removed their hands and stood onlooking. When the shaking stopped, my grandmother stepped forward and slapped me across the face. The room went dark shortly after I fell to the ground.

Chapter 6: Waiting Around Until We Die

I finished my senior year of high school living back at my grandmother's house. I quit all the sports teams and extracurricular activities I was involved with and began working full time so that I could save for an apartment. Each day, I left for school first thing in the morning and after school was finished, I stayed at school and did homework until it was time to go to work at the gas station which was nearby. After work, I went to bed.

Since I wasn't allowed to go back to church, I began working on the weekends too. I applied to 3 colleges—one in state and two out of state, and I got into all 3. For every form that I needed signed, I forged my grandmother's signature and because I memorized her social security number, I kept her completely out of the loop regarding my post-graduation plans. I had one goal: to get out.

I received the most scholarships and financial aid to stay in state, but instead of living on campus, I opted for leasing an apartment with Sammie, my girlfriend, since I needed a place to live immediately after graduation.

That first year of college and working full time was difficult. I was overwhelmed by everything and exhausted all the time. Additionally, halfway through the first semester, I realized that Sammie was only a way out of a bad situation and that I wasn't in love with her. Our personalities began to clash, so I quit working at the gas station and found a job at a restaurant that paid a bit more.

The new job gave me the ability to rent a small apartment closer to school, but by the end of my freshman year of college, I began to slip into a depression. I had a decent apartment, my grades were very good, I liked my job, but I was lonely and disconnected from my community.

I missed my family, my friends and my teachers from high school. I missed my life at church—the programs, the events, the people. Feeling so loved and important because of who my family was and because of everything I got to do gave me a sense of value that was no longer present.

I still prayed and read my Bible, but since the exorcism by the Aunties hadn't worked and I was still attracted to both men and women, I was convinced that I was destined for a lifetime in Hell.

I was miserable inside. I occupied my mind with school and I worked at night and on the weekends.

When the semester ended, and I no longer had homework to distract me, I started partying with some of the guys I worked with and gained access to a different kind of life.

Long days and late nights, and alcohol, cigarettes, marijuana, and food were worthy companions that numbed the pain of being a disappointment and drowned out my fears of death and Hell. By the end of that summer, I forgot sobriety and planned my exit from the world.

I wrote letters to everyone in my family—explaining to them how I tried to change, but couldn't, and that I was deeply hurt by their rejection of me. After writing the letters and placing them into neat piles in front of my apartment door, I packed my belongings into moving boxes and stacked them nearby. If I was doomed to live a life of misery and isolation, then life was not worth living and nothing was worth having.

I concluded that it would be better to die and risk going to Hell than to remain alive. I read from the book of Psalms until I worked up enough courage, and then I prayed and asked God to forgive me either way—for being an abomination if I lived or for killing myself if I died.

I swallowed two handfuls of pills and overdosed on a combination of over-the-counter medication.

****

I drifted awake to find myself surrounded by a bright overhead light and several people. I couldn't hear anything, and I couldn't make out any of their faces, so I asked, "Where am I?"

No one seemed to hear me.

"Why can't I move? Why is no one answering me?" I yelled, blinking hard to clear the shine from my eyes.

I soon realized that I was in a hospital.

"I'm still here? I'm alive?" I cried, surprised and disappointed at my failed suicide attempt. I didn't think I would make it.

I went to great lengths to end my life, and the thought of failure made me panic. I didn't have a plan B because, in my mind, there was no alternative to death. Discovering that I was still alive angered me and I was afraid of what would happen next.

I tried to get up. But my arms and legs were restrained. Frantic, I thrashed and screamed until I drifted back to sleep. When I woke up in the hospital the second time, the room was dark—except for the wide-open doorway. Sitting near the door was a woman in a rocking chair. Her skin was dark, and her hair was pulled back into a bun. I immediately became emotionally moved by the sight of this woman because she looked familiar.

"Mom, is that you?" I asked, surprised and relieved that she was there. It had been years since I'd seen my mother.

"Oh sweet, child..." she said, as she stood up and walked over to my bed.

I groggily sat up on the bed to meet her extended arms, she pulled me in and started caressing my back. I can't remember the last time I felt so safe with my mother.

"Mom, so much has happened—so much has changed over the years. But you're here. I can't believe you're here."

I cried into her soft, warm tenderness the tears of many years and lots of anguish. I had so many questions, but I just wanted to be held by her. I just wanted to know that everything was going to be alright.

"Baby, I'm so sorry," she said. "I'm so sorry things ended up this way for you."

"Mom, why did you stop loving me?" I asked. My breath and the moment were suspended in the air.

"Baby, I'm so sorry. If I was your mom, I sure would love you and you wouldn't be here like this," she said.

I pulled away and looked in the face of the woman who I thought was my mother. She looked like my mom. Sensing my confusion, the woman reached behind the hospital bed and pushed a switch on the wall. Suddenly, an overhead light came on. It wasn't my mother after all. It turns out the woman was a nurse that was sitting with me because I had been placed on suicide watch.

After spending a few days in intensive care, I was transferred to the psychiatric ward of the hospital. There, I was medicated twice daily, participated in several hours of talk therapy, had lots of time for reflection, and my access to the outside world was limited to visiting hours and inbound phone calls. At the end of the first week, I received a phone call.

"Teasha, this is your mom! I don't have much time to talk, so I'll make it fast," she said. Unlike the woman in the hospital, the voice on the other end of the phone was jarring and cold.

"Mom, are you coming to see me?" I desperately wanted to cry as emotion waved through me, but the medication had begun to take effect and a side-effect was the inability to release actual tears—no matter how much I felt them.

"Look, I know that you're in a lot of pain. And I'm sorry. I didn't think it would come to this." My mother sounded impatient.

"Mom, are you coming to see me?" She felt so distant and I felt so drowsy.

"I knew you were different when I was pregnant with you. And you look just like your dad. I didn't expect you to be a girl when you came out and you never acted like one. I was so young then and me and your dad had lots of problems of our own. We just weren't ready for a child like you and I just didn't know things would end up like this. We were so young."

She spoke fast, and I tried to listen to the background noise coming from her end of the phone to determine where she could be calling from.

"So, you're not coming to see me? That's fine. Can you just answer one question for me...?" The question wasn't rhetorical, but I didn't expect an answer. "Why did you stop loving me?" I asked.

"You're trying to tell me that you're in there because of me?!" she shouted. A hearty, sinister laugh vibrated through the telephone receiver.

"Mom that is not what I am saying. There are many reasons why I am here and yes, you are part of it. I know that I am different. I stuffed socks in my underwear, I called myself a boy even though everyone kept telling me I was a girl. I like girls and I like boys. But so do you—you told me so once. I tried really hard to get away from all that and it hasn't worked," I said.

"You tried to beat it out of me every chance you got, and you let Slick do all that stuff to me like you didn't even care. You mocked me—saying I looked like dad. Oh, and dad, when you left dad, he's never been the same since—it's like he stopped living—and he and granny hate me now…"

She then interrupted me and said, "Your daddy was gone long before I left him; he was a lost boy when we got married. You might be smart, Teasha, but there's so much you don't know," she interjected. Her gaze then trailed off into memories.

"Look mom, a lot happened. And you hooked up with Slick and had a kid—and then it was like we didn't even matter. You hated me, and I can't imagine doing to a kid what you guys did to me," I said, feeling anger rise within.

"What the fuck mom…" I screamed, "if it wasn't for granny, I wouldn't have made it this far! She wasn't perfect either, but you didn't even want me. You made that very clear by how you treated me. And then you dropped me off at a bus stop and I don't see you for years…? What kind of mom does that?"

The tears and emotions from all those years tangled up into a ball that was now caught in my throat.

My mother replied, "I didn't call you to listen to all of this, besides, I don't remember things happening like that—the way you say. You're grown now, I get it, you can talk to me however you want! But you didn't have it *that* bad. You want to talk rough—you want to hear what I've been through? I did the best I could with what I had, and what I had wasn't very much."

She continued, "My momma beat me; she had my brothers beat me; I've been raped; your daddy beat me. And Slick. I thought he was different. I didn't know back then what I know now." My mother's voice changed keys between sentences and her tone became softer with each word.

I took a long, deep breath, exhaling into the phone, then said, "Mom, I know your life has been hard. I can't even begin to understand what you've been through, but you are my mom. You gave birth to me and I am sitting on the 5th floor of the very hospital you gave birth to me in because I wanted to end my life. And you don't even come to see me—you call! You can't even own up to what got me in here. I tried to kill myself because everyone has pushed me away, including you. I tried to make everyone happy and I still got pushed aside."

Since the tears were absent, I screamed instead, causing some of the patients who were sitting in hospital gowns beside me on the hard-plastic chairs in the sterile room to move outside of earshot to avoid being emotionally triggered.

"Teasha, you were a special kid and I just wasn't prepared for it. That's all. Do you think I asked for three kids? I was still a baby myself and I had to figure out how to feed you monsters because y'all always needed shit. I had my own living to do and you were too much." Her words were coming quick and their truth pierced me.

"I sacrificed myself to make sure y'all had. You think your granny is so great? If it wasn't for me dropping you off to her, you probably would've died a long time ago," she continued.

"You are serious? So, you would've killed me?" Her words shocked me and deep down I knew they were true.

"I'm just saying, I saved your life and gave you a way out when I dropped you off that night. Yes, life was hard, but it wasn't as bad as you make it sound. I will not remember it like this."

"I can't believe you. You think you're a hero?" My loud voice caught the attention of the hospital aides who were now standing watch beside me.

"I have to get going now. I called because they told me you were in the hospital. I hope you feel better soon," my mother said to me.

I tried to imagine her face. "You're hanging up now that I'm being real with you, but you put up with all that shit from my dad and Slick for years? Do you even love me and my sisters or has it been about you all along?" I asked her.

"If that's what you want to hear, then fine, I love you," she said, and then hung up the phone.

After several seconds of listening to the dial tone, I hung up my line and looked around me. The bright room with chairs in the center had a TV on the far wall that was surrounded by couches. On the other end of the room was the staff counter encased by bulletproof glass.

In the very center of the counter, the glass had a slit through which they slid our medication on a plastic tray with a paper cup filled with water as we each stood in line twice a day to ingest our sanity.

Doors to patient rooms and treatment rooms lined both sides of the rectangular space, and each door had a small, square window and locked from the outside. My room had two twin beds, a fluorescent ceiling light, and a light switch.

There were adults and kids. Patients walking the floors, some rocking in chairs, some sitting alone and talking to themselves, some sitting at the telephone table, some sitting in front of the TV.

My roommate was an older blonde woman who carried around a teddy bear that she talked to incessantly. I later learned from her husband who came to visit often that their baby had died many years ago.

For those patients who had been there the longest, or proved they weren't a threat, they could earn the privilege of wearing their own clothes instead of wearing hospital clothes. I also learned from my roommate's husband that my roommate chose to remain in her hospital gown because it reminded her of the night she gave birth.

The more I talked to and studied the other patients, the more I realized that we were all there because of something that happened to us or around us. We were stuck. I saw so much on the faces of people who, like me, wanted to be happy but were stuck in pain. We were stuck in our minds. A feeling of overwhelming compassion came over me and I started walking around the room.

Talking to my mother on the phone and having her hang up on me, then seeing the faces of the other patients set off a lightbulb in my mind: *I needed to find happiness in spite of my mother and despite my past pain.*

I realized that nothing that had already happened could be undone—no matter how much I screamed. I needed to learn how to release my pain so that I could be unstuck. As these thoughts entered my mind, I felt like a cloud was lifting.

I walked the floor and as I approached each person, I looked into their eyes and whispered a prayer for them. I wanted them and God to know that I saw their pain. That I saw them *beyond* their pain.

Some of the patients spoke back to me as I prayed, some looked past me, and some began to cry as I laid a hand on their arm, held their hands, or sat next to them uttering words from the 23rd Psalm I memorized as a child, "The Lord is my shepherd, I shall not want..."

****

One morning, the following week, I woke up lucid and rested—and not just because of the medication. I slept through the night, for once. And to top it off, I received the news at my evening therapy session the night before, that I earned the privileges of supervised walks outside, my own room, and the use of a notebook and a pencil. Shortly after I finished my breakfast tray this particular morning, I was summoned over the loudspeaker to report to the visiting area.

I arrived in the visiting area of the psych ward to find my grandmother standing gently near the door. "Hi, granny," I said, to the woman in the long, black coat, creased black slacks, and flower-covered white blouse.

She smelled like fall. Her worn black leather purse was hanging off her shoulder and with one hand she gripped several books against her chest. Her peppered black hair curled into a bob and her eyes were pensive yet kind. Her redlined grin reminded me of home. Home after Slick and before exorcisms.

"You look better than you did when they first brought you in," she said, as she put the books on the short oak table beside us. She stretched out her arms and met my shoulders with her hands. We stood there looking into each other's eyes.

"You were here?" I asked, as my head turned downward in shame and surprise.

"Yes," she replied. "I was the first person they called." She placed her purse beside the books and sat down in a chair near the door.

"Who called you?" I asked. The details of the day I arrived in the hospital were blurry.

"The school called," she said. "You showed up for classes that day and ended up in the health center. You were acting funny and talking like you wanted to die. They figured out you took something. They got you to Emergency and called me right away. I'm glad you still have me down as your contact."

Her aging brown eyes began filling with tears as she spoke, "I left work immediately," she went on to say. "And I saw what they did to get all those pills out of you. I've never been so scared in my life—they had you strapped down to the bed and everything!" she cried.

"I can't believe you were here," I said. I appreciated the humility in her gaze.

"Of course, I was here. I came every night you were in the ICU. I'm not surprised you don't remember because you were barely conscious those first nights," she spoke through her tears.

I sat stunned. "I don't know what to say," I said.

"Let me do the talking, you've done enough." Just then, she shuffled through the books beside her. "I brought you a few things, but you won't be here that long. I talked to the doctor and they're going to transfer you to outpatient. They say you're going to be fine. You had the key to your apartment on you when they brought you in...so I stopped by," she said, as she separated the small stack of books.

"You went to my apartment?" I screeched, clearing my throat. "How did you know where I lived?"

I gasped when I remembered the notes and memorial I left behind. When I expected to die, I thought someone would find these things, but I didn't think it would be her since we hadn't spoken in several months and I didn't tell her where I lived.

"I'm no dummy! Yes, I went to your apartment. I got a few things," she said as she placed my journal on the table and opened it.

"There are pages and pages of prayers in here. You begged God to take this away from you—to make you normal. Everything I ever did, I thought it was right, Teasha. I always knew you were different and the church always said people like *that* were evil. But you begged God in these prayers and your spirit is so gentle."

Her voice cracked as the tears flowed. "I know how much you love God," she continued. "The church taught us this was wrong, but I prayed," she said.

"Why would God make you something that would make your own family hate you? Why would God want me to hate my own blood? Teasha, I searched the scriptures for myself, and I prayed. There is something in the Bible for and against everything and all people— and the words were written by other people—I found that out too. I need to ask your forgiveness. God made you this way. God didn't tell me to hate you, my church did. Please forgive me," she begged, as she frantically turned the pages of my journal, not looking up at me.

"Granny, I forgive you. Yes, you hurt me and yes, your rejection of me caused me to lose hope in this life. But you've always been a better mom than even my own mother. You're right, I do love God and I know God for myself. I just wanted to leave this world because I don't fit in it. I know you did your best and the fact that you are here and apologizing to me means more than you'll ever know," I explained.

She looked up at once, the relief under her furrowed brow inspired a single tear to roll out of my right eye onto my cheek.

"You do fit in this world, and you're gonna set a lot of people free. You see, we all look for a leader, and sometimes those leaders only tell us what they learned from other people or from books. You will be a leader that teaches what you learn from life and from God. Baby, I'm sorry I did this to you and my only prayer is that this all be used for God's glory one day," she said, wiping the tears from her eyes with one hand, and sliding my journal across the table with the other hand.

"Here, for what it's worth, I brought your Bible too. I noticed all the markings you wrote in the Psalms…your heart is after God just like David," she said, handing me my Bible.

I felt a shift in our relationship. In that moment, she felt less like a grandma and more like a companion.

"When you get out of here, I want you to come stay with me for a while. When the time is right."

"Ok, I'd like that," I said, truly believing it was all going to be ok.

"And you don't have to work for a while. Give up your apartment and let me take care of you," she pleaded.

"Granny, there's no need for that," I said. "I can still work." I couldn't imagine not having a job.

"Chile, you been working all your life. And trying to live up to everybody's standards on top of getting over all the stuff your mom put you through—you *have* worked," she said. "When you're ready, come stay with me and just take some time for the Spirit to heal your wounds."

"Can I come back to church?" I asked.

"Everybody is welcomed in the house of God, but baby, that church ain't ready yet. If you're gonna be true to yourself and be gay—"

"Granny, I'm not gay," I interrupted.

"Or whatever you are," she said, matter-of-factly. "If you're gonna be true to yourself, you might want to find a church that accepts you. Maybe in time you can go back, but they ain't ready yet. Do you understand what I'm saying to you?"

Her brown almond eyes made me feel warm inside, reminding me of a time right after I moved in with her, and I'd wake up from a nightmare about my mom or Slick.

"Yes ma'am," I said, longing to be held like that 9-year-old child and rocked to sleep.

"Let's pray before I leave," she said, standing up from her chair. "Since you're getting out soon, I won't come back down here, but the moment you leave, you give me a call and tell me where you're at."

She extended her arms, I grabbed her hands, and we bowed our heads.

As she prayed for me, for us, and for the world to be a kinder place for people like me, I couldn't help but think of the last time she prayed for me with the Aunties.

When I was released from the psych ward later that week, I took a leave of absence from school, terminated the lease on my apartment and moved back in with my grandmother.

"Rise and shine and give God the glory!" my grandmother sang. She knocked and then opened the door to my new room in her two-bedroom apartment.

She walked across the square, brown carpeted room and pulled back the heavy curtains she purchased from the hotel furniture liquidation store. She began her retirement from the manufacturing plant some months back, and she downsized and began living alone. The morning sun warmed the cozy, carpeted room that was decorated with a twin bed, 2-shelf bookcase, computer desk, and a black rolling chair that had a cloth seat cushion.

"Good morning, granny," I said groggily. The combination of my prescription sleeping pills and antidepressants, and the days, seemed like brief interruptions from sleep.

"Breakfast is almost ready," she said, standing in the shine from the window with her silky hair combed straight back, and wearing a shimmery thin, white gown and black flip flops. Her eyes were hopeful and humble as the bags underneath them had become more pronounced over the years.

I pulled myself out of the mound of covers atop the too springy mattress and entered the hallway. The smell of coffee and biscuits quickened me. I assumed there was gravy and I went down the hall into the bathroom to wash my face.

While in the bathroom standing at the sink, I heard my grandmother shout from the kitchen over the spraying metal faucet, "I'm only making enough eggs for me since you said they make you nauseous."

The tiny bathroom with all new fixtures was much nicer than our old bathroom. With all of us grandchildren being of working age or college age, my grandmother could finally afford to live someplace nice because she no longer had to financially support anyone but herself.

"Granny, it's the smell that makes me nauseous now, not the eggs themselves," I shouted back. "I think it's a side effect of the medicine. But that's fine. There is gravy though, right?" I asked, as I hung up my washcloth on one of the sparkling silver hooks behind the door.

"Yes, there is," she said, as I retreated toward her voice.

Looking slightly mangled from sleep and wearing my bathrobe and slippers, I entered the kitchen to see my grandmother standing at the stove stirring the contents of the saucepan. Two cups of steaming black coffee were waiting on the counter beside her.

Reaching for the coffee cup I decided was mine, I then asked, "Granny, do I have time for a smoke or is the food ready now?"

"Lord, chile, I wish you didn't smoke those cigarettes," she said, turning around to see me standing in the doorway. "I know your nerves are shot so I get it, but I still don't like that you started smoking. The gravy is almost ready, then I'll start my eggs. Everything else is warming," she said.

"So, I have some time," I said, with a big, toothy grin. "I will be out on the porch." I grabbed my cup of coffee from the countertop that was neatly organized with an electric can opener, a mixer, a toaster, a wooden cutting board, and a black-handled knife set.

I shuffled across the smooth vinyl floor to retrieve my menthol cigarettes and lighter from the brown lacquered kitchen table that was also purchased from the hotel furniture liquidation store.

Taking in long puffs of the tainted air helped me relax my mind and I felt present. My suicide attempt made my grandmother's disdain for my smoking and the anti-smoking warning ad on the side of the cigarette box seem ironic.

When I finished my cigarette, I went inside to help my grandmother plate our food; then we prayed and ate breakfast. For several weeks this was our morning routine.

****

"Granny, are you awake?" I whispered, as I lightly knocked on my grandmother's bedroom door.

My reimbursement check from the security deposit I paid for my apartment had finally come in the mail and I spent that afternoon shopping for clothes while she napped.

"Yes, I'm awake, come on in," she said as I opened the door to her bedroom that was covered in flower patterns from the wall paper to the comforter on her bed.

The temperature in her room always seemed warmer than it was in the rest of the apartment. She was laying in her bed amidst some magazines not watching the television that was turned down low and sitting on top of the dresser directly across from her queen-sized bed.

"What do you think?" I asked.

Until that point, my grandmother had only seen me "dressed up" in skirts and dresses. I stood in her doorway wearing a navy suit coat, faded blue jeans, a white t-shirt, and a black belt to match my black combat boots. My head was filled with skinny, brown and black dyed dreadlocks that didn't quite reach my shoulders.

"So, I see you have new clothes. You look like a boy. Is that the look you're going for?" she said, looking down over her red-framed bifocals. She then shifted her weight to her elbows in a raised plank position on the bed.

"Granny, I am just trying to look more like me," I said, suddenly embarrassed by my decision to knock on her door.

Just as I considered turning around and leaving, she said, "Fix your collar in the back." Her eyes suddenly relaxed and she smiled at me. "It's your birthday, where are you going tonight?"

"We are going to a new LGBTQ bar in town," I replied. "I get free drinks because it's my 21st birthday." I smiled wide as I straightened the collar on my suit coat.

Although I took a leave of absence from school, I kept in touch with two girls from campus and they insisted that I go with them for my birthday and focus on having fun. I wasn't too concerned that we were going to a bar because I was just looking forward to being around people like me—other Lesbian, Gay, Bisexual, Transgender and Queer people.

"Now you be careful at this bar," my grandmother said, as concern flashed across her face. "People do crazy stuff out in this world. I don't like you drinking but I can't stop you. Your granddaddy drank socially. Hell, he drank socially and privately. Just don't leave your drink unattended because anyone could spike it and next thing you know, you'll end up on the news missing or something." Her face relaxed into soft brown wrinkles.

"Granny, no one is going to spike my drink and I won't be kidnapped," I said, sighing and rolling my eyes halfheartedly.

"Just be careful. You remember Ms. Pickens from church? Her son went to a bar many years ago and someone put something in his drink and he's never been the same since," she said, shaking her head in disbelief. "That poor man had his whole life ahead of him. Gone!"

"Granny, I won't leave my drink," I reassured her, shifting my weight on my feet as my back leaned into the doorframe.

"And don't do drugs or have sex with anybody there! You never know what kind of diseases people have," she exclaimed.

"Granny, I might not be acquainted with the bar scene," I smirked, "but I'm pretty sure I'll steer clear of the people doing drugs and having sex there." I let out a huge laugh. "Besides, I've smoked weed before."

"You smoked that stuff?" she screamed, taking off her glasses to see me more clearly.

Our gaze was undisturbed.

"Yes," I replied. "Last year I smoked quite a bit. I'm not proud of it but I'm not ashamed of it either. It got me through a really difficult time."

Neither of us moved or blinked for what felt like forever but only a minute or so had passed.

"I'm really happy that our relationship is being restored," she said, "but I don't know how much more honesty I can take today. You're standing here looking like a man, I can accept that. You're going to a bar—a gay one at that, ok. And now you tell me you did drugs. Sounds like true confessions; anything else you want to tell me to put me in an early grave?" Her wide smile tried to mask her panic.

"No, there's nothing else I want to confess at this point, but I am proud of you. Two years ago, I could've told you this and you probably would've tried to kill me," I said, laughing for us both.

"I'm not proud of that, but you're probably right," she said, folding up her magazines and sitting up on the bed. "What time will you be in?"

"Honestly, I'm not sure," I replied. "If it's too late, I might stay out until the morning; I don't want to wake you up. I can stay the night at Casey and Dee's dorm room."

"Chile, I'll probably be up anyway. I go to the bathroom seems like all night long these days," she said, chuckling. "You come on back anytime and don't worry about me. Just enjoy the night and be safe."

My grandmother's guilt from me ending up in the hospital made her a bit overprotective but it was quite refreshing to be more of my authentic self around her.

"Thanks, granny," I said as I walked over to her bed and leaned over to kiss her on the cheek.

I was surprised at how well she handled our conversation. As I walked back toward the door, I turned to look at her, and her face seemed brighter than before.

"Happy birthday, baby," she said.

"Thanks, granny," I replied, closing her bedroom door.

Chapter 7: Suddenly

After showing the security guard my identification card, I entered the split-level bar and was greeted by music, flashing neon signs, small round tables with chairs huddled around them, and most surprisingly, clean floors. I have a thing for clean floors.

The place was packed wall-to-wall with people of all shades and from various walks of life. There was a drink serving station directly across the room. I don't quite know what I expected but after I scanned the room, I felt welcomed and was able to relax comfortably into the atmosphere.

My friends and I made our way through the crowd and headed upstairs to the dance floor. It was hard to see, and it was even harder to hear anyone's conversation over the booming pop tunes, so while my friends got comfortable and started dancing near the stage, I ventured back downstairs. I spotted a swivel chair at the bar and made my way over to it.

As I waited for the bartender to check my identification card that I placed on the polished cherry wood countertop, my eyes caught the face of a woman who had just entered the room. She had long brown hair and was wearing a fitted black cocktail dress.

She had high cheekbones and her olive skin looked as if it had been kissed by the sun. Her curvy physique filled her dress in all the right places. She was the most beautiful woman I had ever seen.

This mystery woman took my breath away and my jaw hit the floor. I don't know how long it had been, but I caught myself staring at her with my mouth hanging open when I realized that she was staring back at me and laughing at me. I immediately became mortified.

I grabbed my ID from the counter and ran upstairs to find my friends. Casey and Dee cackle-laughed between songs as I recounted the tale of the beautiful laughing woman from across the room. They ordered me another drink to calm my nerves since I didn't get my free birthday drink downstairs.

I warmed the wall with my back while my friends danced, sipping my drink and chain smoking cigarettes. After a few songs, I spotted the beautiful woman from downstairs at the back of the room.

I watched her walk across the dance floor and sit down at a table near the stage. New nerves bubbled up within me, and I decided that I had to speak to this mystery woman. I put out my cigarette, quickly chugged the remainder of my Sex on the Beach, and then made my way through the crowd to her table.

"Excuse me miss," I said, as I sat down in the empty chair beside her. "I saw you downstairs and I might have been staring, and I just want to apologize for that. It is not my intention to objectify you." I leaned in close and spoke loudly over the music, hoping she heard and forgave me.

"Yes, I caught that," she said, grinning. "It was kind of sweet. Tell you what, when a song comes on that I like, I'll come find you and we can dance." Her amber lipstick smile was wide and perfect, and she smelled like softness.

"Really? I mean, ok," I said, clearing my throat. "I'll be right over there." I pointed across the dancefloor to the wall where my friends were now huddled looking at us. "So, when you hear that song just come on over." I spoke with coolness as my stomach dropped with butterflies.

"Alright, stay close," she said, smiling as I stood up from the table. "My name is Diane by the way." She extended her porcelain hand and I shook it loosely.

I walked back to my spot against the wall to replay for my friends the conversation between Diane and me. They roared with laughter when I realized that I hadn't remembered to give her my name.

Diane and I did dance that night—and not just for one song, but three. I remembered to give her my name, and at the end of our last dance, she gave me her phone number.

I promised to call her.

Just as she predicted, my grandmother was awake and getting out of the bathroom when I got back home later that night.

While walking past me in the hallway, she said through a sleepy smile, "How was your night? You're alive and you don't look high on drugs; so that's good."

"Granny, I didn't go to the bar to do drugs," I roared! My laughter startled her, and she flinched. "My night was amazing," I said. "I think I'm in love." I leaned against the oak frame of her dimly lit room with glistening eyes.

"What do you mean?" she said, sitting down on the edge of her queen-sized bed.

"It was like the saying, 'love at first sight'." I said, as I took the slip of paper with Diane's number out of my pocket and stared at it.

"And you're talking about a woman?" she asked. She climbed back into the cozy bed and swung her feet under a thick flower-covered comforter.

"Yes ma'am," I replied, nearly star struck. "She is the most beautiful woman I've ever seen. We danced all night and she is so kind." My words oozed, and the switching on of my grandmother's bedside lamp revealed my grin.

"Now come on," she said. "How can you be this smitten? You met the woman at a bar and y'all danced. And now you're in love?" She spoke while fluffing her pillows.

"Granny, I am so serious. It's like I've known her before even though I don't know her at all, and I just want to get to know her even more," I confessed. "I could've danced with her all night! She is so beautiful. Her olive skin, it is like silk and her long, brown hair smells so nice. And it is soft! Her eyes are deep—they are a brownish green color. Her teeth are big, and she smiles from her soul. She is unlike anyone I've *ever* met before."

I closed my eyes, leaned my head against the doorframe and replayed the last dance we had together. I got to put my arms around Diane's waist during that last dance.

"My Lord!" my grandmother gasped. She then took a drink from the water glass on her nightstand. "She got you talking so much you made my mouth dry—I need a drink!", she exclaimed. "You should've brought home some of whatever it was you were drinking for me!" She laughed heartily.

"Oh ha-ha, aren't you funny!" I said, before plopping down on the bed. "Granny, she is amazing...I don't even know her last name and I saw my future with her!"

I looked down at Diane's name and number again, this time trying to make conclusions about her personality and character by analyzing her handwriting. She spelled her name in all caps and her letters were all the same size and evenly spaced. I wondered, based on her handwriting, if she was controlling or overly concerned with physical appearances.

"Chile, you ain't been gay long enough to be this in love and thinking about a future with somebody," my grandmother said. "Don't you want to spend some time getting to know yourself before you think about getting hooked up with some woman?" Her gaze stiffened. "You just got out of the hospital a couple of months ago and your mind still ain't right, yet. You got more healing to do."

"Granny—I know that you're trying, and I appreciate it," I said. "But I am not gay. I'm not gay or straight, I'm queer." I folded the slip of paper then tucked it into my jacket pocket.

"Gay's the word I have, so that's the word I use," she said with a serious tone. "I ain't calling you no queer—where I'm from, queers and sissies get beat up. All I'm saying is, you should wait. You don't know enough about this lifestyle yet. How many women have you been with?" Her inquisitive eyes peered into me.

"Ok, no," I contested. "I am not answering that." I laid back on her bed, dramatically throwing my body across her lap, and I covered my face in horror.

"You've been telling me everything else—I can handle it," she said. "I won't be upset or judge you. We're past that—I'm just trying to learn," she said. "How many women have you been with? More than 5 or less than 5?"

"Granny, I am not doing this. I don't want to know how many people you've slept with; I don't even want to think of you as someone who has had sex. I can't have this conversation with you," I said, embarrassed. Although I was mortified by our topic of conversation, I was encouraged by my grandmother's ability to ask this question.

"It's been more than 5—is that why you won't answer?" she asked.

"Granny—no! It has not been more than 5. Jesus Christ! Do you think I'm some sort of whore? Wait, don't answer that," I said, springing up from the bed with excitement.

"Watch your mouth. You're the one who won't answer; what am I supposed to think if you don't want to answer? I'm just curious," she said rather sheepishly.

"2. I've been with 2 women." My face flushed as I let out a deep sigh and dropped my shoulders.

"Only 2? You're attractive; I thought more than that. How many men have you been with?" She smiled, and her eyes perked open a bit more.

"I'm going to bed. Goodnight." I leaned in to kiss her on the cheek and she grabbed my face with both her hands.

"I'm trying. Meet me halfway," she said, smiling softly.

My eyes filled with tears from the warmth of her hands. I closed them, let out a deep sigh and said, "1." I removed her hands from my face and sat back down next to her on the bed.

"So how do you know if you're gay—I mean, how do you know you're this way if you've only been with one guy?" she asked.

"Granny, did you know you liked men before you met granddaddy?" I asked back.

"Of course!" She smirked.

"It's just like that. I don't have to have sex with someone to know that I am attracted to them. Whether I have sex with someone or not doesn't determine whether I am attracted to them, and just because I've enjoyed sex with a man doesn't mean I can't enjoy sex with a woman," I said, shocked at the words coming out of my mouth.

"So how do you know if you're attracted to someone?" she asked, with a puzzled look on her face.

"You get a funny feeling inside. You want to look at them, sit next to them, listen to them talk, be close... You know—like I'm sure you felt about granddaddy back in the day."

"And you have that feeling for women?" she asked, contemplatively.

"Yes, and men too." I maintained eye contact with her.

She gasped, "I just can't imagine feeling that way about another woman!"

"That just means you're a heterosexual." I smiled.

"Honestly, I lived in a different time and we didn't even entertain the idea of anything else. When you got old enough, you found a man that you got along with and you married him. I wasn't thinking about being close to nobody, I just knew it was time for me to be married."

She looked away reminiscing.

"Granny, it's not too late—you might meet someone that you want to be close to. I mean, come on, granddaddy's been dead for a long time. Maybe you should get back out there!" I fell back against the bed again, this time, laughing.

"I'm too old to be thinking about going back out anywhere and I sure as hell am too old to be thinking about switching teams. I'm perfectly fine being a heterosexual. I wouldn't even know what to do with a woman." She turned her face toward me and released a deep guttural laugh.

"Before you ask any more questions, I am going to get up and go to bed now. Goodnight granny, and thanks for this chat. I love you." I stood up, kissed her on the cheek, and hugged her neck.

"I love you too," she said, still laughing, as I left the room. "See you in the morning."

****

Diane and I talked on the phone several times a day and we began spending all our free time together. Depression's fog was lifting, and I was slowly integrating back into society. I decided to extend my leave of absence from school through the following semester and to feel productive, I found another job working overnights in the stockroom of a high-end retail store.

Since my grandmother was driving less, she didn't mind me taking her car, and several nights a week, I drove to Diane's suburban apartment for dinner before heading into work.

"We should have a dinner party," Diane said to me one evening. "Wouldn't it be great if our families became friends?"

On this night at Diane's spacious one-bedroom apartment decorated by lavender incense, acoustic guitar music and everything do-it-yourself, we cooked dinner together. Boneless and skinless chicken breasts, asparagus, macaroni and cheese, and potato salad. The ritual of cooking was our time to catch up on the day's events as we spoke over the Lilith tunes soothing from the stereo.

"I'm not sure that's such a good idea. Driving to the suburbs for a dinner party hosted by an interracial lesbian couple might be a stretch for most, if not all, of my family members," I said before sipping from my glass of red wine.

"Come on, that's so harsh. I love your family! And your granny really likes me. It seems like her and my mom would get along well because they both have great senses of humor."

Diane's voice from the dining room as she was setting the table sounded sweet; she meant well. She was wearing oversized cotton pajama pants, a V-neck t-shirt that hung loosely around her shoulders and her long hair was tossed together in a bun. In a black jogging suit and cotton crew socks, I stirred the melting cheese in the saucepan on the stove.

"You haven't met my whole family. My grandmother does like you, but she has done some internal work that most of my other family members haven't done yet. They're still pretty bigoted. Your skin color alone challenges their ignorance. I told you how my family responded to finding out my sexuality. My family is just different than yours. And if it's up to me, you'll never meet my parents."

"I'm not white," Diane said, banging a plate against the dining room table.

"Honey, I know you're not white, but you have long, straight brown hair and your skin is very light. To my family, you will be considered white." I put the spoon down onto the spoon rest, went into the dining room, stood behind her and placed my arms around her waist. "Things in my family are pretty much black and white, gay or straight. There is nothing in between."

"What difference does it make what color my skin is or what gender I am? Love is love. Why can't people just be happy that we found each other?" She rested her head back against my shoulder.

"Because some people are ignorant. Some people are hateful. Some people are too afraid to open their minds. Some people only think what they need to think in order to escape religious condemnation…" I said, releasing a heavy sigh.

"I just don't get it. At the end of the day, isn't blood thicker than all this other stuff? We're all human. I will never understand how people can be divided because of skin color or sexuality when we all have the same color blood flowing through our veins." Diane was frustrated.

"Yes, but like my grandmother says, some people just aren't ready. They aren't ready to be challenged. They aren't ready to let go of what they thought was the truth to embrace another truth. They aren't ready to be wrong." I leaned my head back, closed my eyes, and inhaled the seasoned air.

"Maybe our first dinner party can just be for friends then," she said. A half-hearted smile flashed across Diane's face, I kissed her cheek and went into the kitchen to check on the food.

The following spring, I resumed my college coursework and moved in with Diane because balancing work schedules with class times meant that we would hardly see each other if we continued to live apart.

"We should wear matching outfits," Diane said, a huge smile twinkled in her eyes.

It was a humid evening, and Diane and I invited over friends for dinner. We were sitting outside on the screened-in porch eating Thai and drinking sangrias when she asked if we could attend this year's Gay Pride festival. Sitting beside each other in plastic lawn chairs, her thin, pale legs were draped across mine.

"Matching outfits—do you honestly think we can find something to wear that we both like?" I laughed at the absurdity of her suggestion.

"It's Pride—everyone who is someone will be there! Wouldn't it be cute if we dressed alike?"

The warm breeze was blowing her hair across her face so as Diane smiled at me, she twisted her hair up into a bun with one of the scrunchy binders she often wore around her wrist.

"Honey, you're more of a girly girl, and I don't think you'll be comfortable dressing like me."

My friends and I laughed at the thought of Diane wearing loose jeans and bigger t-shirts like I frequently wore. Although Diane wore jeans and t-shirts for her construction job, she enjoyed wearing clothes like dresses, sleeveless tank tops, fitted pants, and shorts cut above the knee when she wasn't at work.

"Don't you get tired of looking like a tomboy? I mean, you're so beautiful. You should dress up some time," she said, as she relaxed back into her chair.

"You don't like the way I dress?" I asked, placing my drink down on the small plastic table that was in the center of us holding our beverages and dinner.

"I love you. And I just want us to dress up together—it will be fun!" Diane's brownish green eyes flickered in the night.

"Whatever we decide on has to include me wearing pants—I won't budge on that. I don't wear shorts and I will not wear a skirt," I insisted.

My voice was adamant, and my friends teased and chuckled at the thought of me wearing a dress. We continued our conversation about many things that evening, and this was my first time getting the impression that deep-down, Diane wasn't happy with my physical appearance.

For several weeks we went back and forth until Diane and I were able to decide on clothes to wear to the Gay Pride festival. We wore matching blue jeans and black spaghetti-strapped shirts. I was satisfied by the pants and I secretly hated the shirts, but I wanted her to be happy, so I compromised.

When we arrived at the Gay Pride festival, my discomfort only intensified as several thousand people were swarming through the booths and tables that were stationed along the edges of the park on that hot and muggy day. I imagined a few hundred people—like at the LGBTQ bar we now frequented. But the sight of several thousand people was much more than my introverted nature could handle.

Men wearing leather outfits, women in cargo shorts and tank tops, families pushing strollers of dangling kids, people with their pets on leashes, children splashing in nearby sprinklers, loud music, a game of pickup basketball on one of the courts, a volleyball game across the park in the sand, police officers serving as security on bicycles and riding horses, food truck vendors filling the air with smells from foods like burgers, corn dogs, cotton candy, gyros, and French fries, and several people singing peace songs with locked arms at the park entrances to drown out the anti-gay chants from the religious extremists who were there in protest.

"Isn't this great?" Diane said with excitement as we made our way through the crowd. We stopped at every table, booth, tent, and station to eye their wares.

"No, not really. There's a lot going on and there's so many people," I said. I was hot, overstimulated, and anxious about my spaghetti-strapped shirt that kept riding up.

"Oh relax," Diane said. "You can *be* you here. Where else can we walk around like this in the middle of the day, surrounded by people just like us, and be proud of being alive? This is fun!"

She grabbed my hand and pulled me through the crowd. As we made our way through the park viewing the displayed art, handmade jewelry, books on everything from relationship advice to estate planning, and pamphlets from community organizations and local businesses, I noticed a tent with a rainbow cross on it.

My mind flashed immediately to the cross embossed onto the communion wafers I used to receive at my old church when I was a kid.

"Let's go over here," I said.

My sudden stop nearly yanked Diane's hand off her arm. I pivoted toward the tent and pulled Diane beside me. When we got to the tent, a familiar comfort washed over me.

"Hi there, how are you ladies doing today?"

We were greeted by the cheerful voice of a petite African American woman who was smiling wide, seated behind the table. Her hair was in tight curls and she was wearing a fitted pink shirt with a matching pleated skirt, like a cheerleader's outfit.

The plastic white table top was sprinkled with chocolate candy, rubber bracelets, several stacks of postcards, business cards and pamphlets; and there was a clipboard on each end of the table that had pens holding down the forms requesting contact information.

"We are good! How are you?" I said. "Are you from a Christian church?" I had never heard of a church that welcomed LGBTQ people before.

"I am great, and yes, I am from a Christian church." The woman stood up and handed me one of the pamphlets from the table. "Do you have a church home?" she asked.

"I used to, but I haven't gone for a few years…" My voice trailed off and I didn't notice Diane wander away from the table as I read the church information.

"You should come check us out sometime. My spouse is the pastor. She should be right back if you want to stick around awhile." The pastor's wife had an energetic and encouraging spirit about her that made me more curious about the church.

"No, we should probably go," I said, as I turned to discover Diane standing at another table several feet away.

"Ok, well here is information for our services, and a flier for our upcoming event. We are having church service on a yacht at the end of the summer, you should bring your girlfriend and anyone else who is interested."

She handed me a tri-fold informational pamphlet and a glossy postcard that had a picture of a boat in the middle of it surrounded by clustered cutouts of brown faces that I assumed belonged to the members of the church. I turned over the postcard to discover the event information:

> Full Truth Fellowship Presents: Church on the Water
>
> Sunday, August 24, 2003
>
> Lake Minnetonka
>
> 10am

"Thank you for being here. I look forward to the event." I tucked the postcard and pamphlet into my back pocket and made my way to the end of the table to write my contact information down on one of the clipboards.

The idea of this church excited me. I couldn't wait to tell Diane about the upcoming event—we both loved the water. I navigated my way over to Diane who was thumbing through large poster prints from a local artist that were on display.

"Why did you leave?" I asked her.

"Oh, I'm not really interested in the church thing; I thought it best to let you have that time." Diane turned to face me and seemed genuinely content.

"The church thing? I wish you would've stayed. They have an event coming up—service on a yacht—I want us to go!" I said. I then retrieved the folded postcard from my pocket and thrusted it at her with excitement.

"I don't know," she said, glancing down at the ad. "Church really isn't my thing."

"Come on, it will be great! I have waited for years to find a church that would accept me. And I've never been on a yacht before, it will be so wonderful if you went with me. I don't want to go alone," I pleaded.

"I know that church was really important to you growing up and I want you to have that again," Diane said, her eyes softening. "Sure, I'll go with you."

I grabbed the postcard and stuffed it back into my pocket. I then pulled Diane close and rested my head in the crook of her neck and exhaled.

****

There was one white lesbian couple, one man, 4 kids and about 2 dozen women on the yacht that morning as we sailed across the lake listening to the inspired words and gospel tunes. Diane and I were the only mixed-race couple, and other than the kids who were sitting up front next to the pastor's wife, we were among the youngest in a crowd of 30- and 40- somethings.

It was a simple service. A small gospel choir sang acapella in between prayers and scripture reading, and the charismatic pastor preached a dynamic sermon and invited us all to return the following week to the church's regular worship service.

It was so peaceful to float across the waves with the sun shining down on us and I felt the presence of God surrounding me. I knew that I wanted to return the next week and I was eager to know what Diane thought of the experience.

"Why can't they just be women?" Diane asked, as we left the boat and returned to our car.

"What do you mean by that?" I said, sensing the frustration in her voice.

"Those couples are just so stereotypical—one has to look all butch like a man and one has to be extra feminine. Why can't they just be women?" Diane said, driving us home in our green sedan.

"Why does it bother you so much if they are comfortable with who they are?" I asked, defensively.

"It's hard enough being a lesbian in a world that tells us we are inferior to men and then you have these women who go around trying to look like men when they're not men. I get being comfortable—not everyone needs to be in heels and skirts but some of the women at this church have buzz cuts and wear men's suits—if I didn't know any better, I'd say they wanted to *be* men." A look of disgust covered Diane's face as she spoke.

"What if they did? What if some of them do want to be men, or felt like they were men, or some sort of male-female hybrid—and this is just them expressing themselves?" I said, just as a sickening feeling tightened in the pit of my stomach. Diane wasn't the only one feeling disgusted.

"We were born women—with breasts, vaginas and hips. I'm a lesbian because I am attracted to other women, not a woman who dresses and acts like a man. I might as well be bisexual or straight if I'm gonna be sitting there hugged up with a woman who looks like a man." Diane's face turned a deep red.

"Do I embarrass you by the way I dress?" I asked, closing my eyes and resting my head back against the seat. I began to focus on my breath and the sound of the tires hitting the road beneath us.

"I'm glad we found the church because I know how happy it makes you to be connected to church again, but I look at some of these couples and I just don't want that to become us," she said. "I love being a woman. I love my hair, I love smelling good, I love wearing makeup and dressing up like a girl. I love being a girl and I wish you did too, but if you feel like you need to look less feminine to be comfortable, I'm sure we can compromise."

"I don't want to lose you and I don't want you to be uncomfortable with me," I said, swallowing hard to suppress the part of myself that knew my feeling like a boy would never go away.

"I'm not uncomfortable with you—I'm uncomfortable with women who *have* to look like men." Diane's right hand left the steering wheel and she placed it on my knee. "I will always love you," she said.

I sat in silence.

"What are you thinking about?" she asked.

"I can't imagine my life without you," I answered dryly, still with my eyes closed.

"Then don't try to…I want us to be together forever," she said. I opened my eyes to see a bright smile dance across her face, then Diane turned her hand over on my knee as if she wanted me to grab it, so I did. We held hands in silence for the rest of the car ride home.

Chapter 8: Epiphany

Our new pastor, Pastor Blake, was a broad woman with a deep voice and a peppered-gray faded haircut. With her height and build, she resembled an all-star basketball player. She and her wife had become really supportive friends to Diane and me since we joined the church and began attending weekly services.

Each church service began with a song and prayer led by the congregation, and then the pastor read the scripture and began her sermon.

"God is good," the pastor shouted into the podium mic.

"All the time," the congregation responded.

"And all the time?" the pastor inquired.

"God is good," we responded.

It felt so good to be in a church surrounded by people who were just like me. People who knew the struggle of being disconnected from the traditional Black church because of our sexual orientation and people who didn't fit neatly into traditional white churches because of the color of our skin.

Nearly 4 dozen of us gathered in the gymnasium of an elementary school each Sunday afternoon. Sitting in metal folding chairs clothed in our Sunday's best—some wore creased blue jeans and large sweatshirts, some skirts and dresses, and some folks wore suits. We received inspired words that made me dream of peace and hope for a prosperous future.

After church this particular Sunday, I asked Pastor Blake if Diane and I could briefly meet with her, and she obliged.

"Thanks for your time today, pastor, and thank you for your message," I said, as I arranged three chairs in a corner of the gymnasium for us. The fitted black turtleneck sweater I was wearing felt especially tight around my neck as mild anxiety flushed through me.

"You know these messages are as much for me as they are for y'all?" Pastor Blake spoke humbly as she sat down in one of the metal folding chairs. "And how are you, Diane?" she asked, unbuttoning the collar of her robe.

Diane smiled as she sat down, crossed her legs at the knee, and took my hand. "I am great, thanks for asking," she said, as she gathered her hair and shifted it to the front of one shoulder.

Diane was wearing a flowery, silk blouse and fitted, tan dress pants that hugged her hips. Her tall, brown leather boots made her legs look longer than they were.

"What brings you two here to talk?" the pastor asked. "Is everything ok? It's been great having you active in church."

A look of concern covered the pastor's face as she unzipped the black preacher's robe to the waist and took a white handkerchief from the breast pocket of her navy-blue vest. She then wiped the sweat from her forehead.

"I wanted us to meet with you because we've been together for a while, and we see our future together, but we need some advice on how to make some compromises for the relationship," I explained as I squeezed Diane's hand.

"What kind of compromises?" Pastor Blake inquired.

"It's mainly about appearances and presentation," I shared. "Diane is uncomfortable with how I dress, I want to make her happy, and I don't think I should be expected to dress differently to make her happy?" I sighed deeply.

"It's not just about that—I am making compromises too," Diane said, letting go of my hand.

"Ok, what's wrong with the way Teasha dresses, Diane?" Pastor Blake asked. She shifted in her chair to face Diane.

"I am making compromises too, so this is not one sided," Diane retorted.

"What's wrong with how she dresses and what compromises are you making for the relationship?" Pastor Blake was focused solely on Diane and not looking at me when she spoke this time.

"For starters, I am not a church person—I mean, I believe in God and everything, but we've been coming here every Sunday for months because this is important to her," Diane said, looking at me.

"I feel like if I can make this kind of compromise, then she can make some compromises too," she said.

"Ok…" Pastor Blake shot a glance toward me. "So, what are you asking her to do that she won't do?" she asked Diane.

"It's not that I am asking her to do anything that she won't do. She does it for the most part, but I know she isn't comfortable," Diane pleaded.

"She's talking about my clothes and the way I dress," I lamented. "She doesn't like me wearing masculine clothes all the time, so I've been mixing it up and trying to be more feminine," I said.

"And what's wrong with her dressing in masculine clothes?" the pastor asked. "Are you uncomfortable with women who wear masculine clothes?" Pastor Blake's eyes ceased smiling and her light brown cheeks flushed.

"I would just like her to look more like a girl sometimes," Diane said, lowering her head.

"Are you uncomfortable with me—I dress *very* masculine?" Pastor Blake asked, her voice raising slightly.

"If that's you, that's you…I just want the woman I am going to spend the rest of my life with to look like a woman," Diane answered.

"And *I* want the woman I am going to spend the rest of my life with to be a Christian," I snapped back.

"Let me ask you both a question. Diane, when you and Teasha went on your first date, what did she have on?"

Diane laughed nervously and replied, "She was actually dressed pretty similarly to how she is dressed now. She was wearing loose blue jeans—but they weren't baggy, and she had on a black turtleneck sweater."

"Ok," Pastor Blake said, turning to me. "Teasha, when you first met Diane, was she a Christian?"

"She said she went to church as a kid but hadn't really gone much as an adult," I said, feeling defeated.

"So, you both met each other one way, and now you're trying to make each other be something different. Am I getting this right?" Pastor Blake had a puzzled look.

"When you put it like that, it sounds kind of ridiculous," I said, as I lowered my head into my hands.

"We love each other, we do want to be together, and we are willing to try to make it work," I heard Diane say.

"Yes, it's very clear that you love each other but what I want to know is if you love yourselves? Teasha—with all due respect, if you loved yourself, you would dress and look however you feel comfortable. And Diane, if you loved yourself, you would come to church because you want to be here not because you feel like you have to please Teasha."

"So, what do we do pastor?" I asked. I couldn't bear the thought of losing myself or Diane at this point.

"That's for you two to decide. Whatever you do, make sure you are honoring the truth of who God inspires you to be," the pastor replied. "We get one life to live and you must figure out, if you live this life together, whether you can compromise who you are or accept each other for who you are. Whatever you decide, you're the ones who have to be ok and live with the consequences."

"We are talking about clothes!" Diane shouted. "What is so hard about wearing feminine clothes sometimes? You *are* a female!"

"That's just it though...I don't feel like a girl," I cried. "I am not even comfortable calling myself one. I can wear the clothes; I can put on makeup; I can walk in heels. It just doesn't feel right. None of it! I did all that for years for my grandmother and it just isn't me," I said.

"But I've seen you wear feminine clothes and you look comfortable to me," Pastor Blake interjected.

"I can play the part, that's not a problem. And if it were just about clothes, it wouldn't be a big deal to wear feminine clothes every once in a while," I explained.

"I'm doing that now. I just don't want to be expected to dress a certain way and I don't want her looking disgusted with me on the days I don't wear girl's clothes," I said defensively.

"Diane, are you disgusted with Teasha?" the pastor asked.

"She doesn't disgust me. I was a tomboy—I hated wearing girl's clothes! But I grew out of that phase as I got older. I guess I'm just hoping she does too. She is a very attractive woman and I just want to show that off more," Diane said, turning toward me and smiling with tears filling her eyes.

I turned toward Diane and grabbed her hands. "Baby, I love you," I said. "I can wear the clothes, but I need for you to understand that I don't feel the same way about being a girl like you do. It's not just about clothes, I literally cannot relate to being a woman. I know how I was born, but ever since I was a little kid, I never thought of myself as a female."

"It sounds like you're a stud to me," Pastor Blake interrupted.

"What's a stud?" I asked, confused.

"A stud is a masculine lesbian," the pastor replied.

"But I am more queer than lesbian—I like girls and guys," I said.

A puzzled look came over Pastor Blake's face and her jaw dropped, "I didn't know that," she said. "I've only seen you with Diane, so I just thought you were a straight up dyke."

My eyes got wide hearing her say the word, *dyke* because I thought it was only used in derogatory circumstances.

"I'm just attracted to the soul of a person," I said. "I don't care what gender they are or how they dress. I look at the inside. And I guess that's what I wish Diane could feel for me." I returned my gaze back to Diane, "I wish you could just love me for me regardless of what I wear."

"And that's my point too..." Diane said. "If clothes don't matter and you can see past the outside of a person, then what difference does it make whether or not you dress more feminine?"

"I truly enjoyed sitting down with you both," Pastor Blake interrupted, "but I need to get going because my wife and kids are waiting for me."

"I am going to pray that you two find clarity. You have some decisions to make but don't move too fast—give yourselves some time. Whatever you decide, just make sure that you are both proud of who you are and who you're with. We can't make anybody be what they are not; your only responsibility is to live in the full truth of who God has called you to be."

Pastor Blake stood up with her robe now half unzipped and extended her right hand to us both. I got up first to shake it and then Diane got up shortly afterward. As she walked away, and I listened to her footsteps echo across the gymnasium floor, I couldn't help but think within myself, *"God, who are you calling me to be?"*

Chapter 9: Transition

"Teasha, you there?" My grandmother called me on a crisp March afternoon on my cell phone as I was walking between classes along the cobblestone streets of my Midwestern liberal arts college. The wind was blowing hard that day as the last remnants of winter echoed through the breeze.

"Yes, I'm here," I said. "Hi granny, how are you?" Since I moved in with Diane, my grandmother and I spoke by phone often, and she was always eager to hear about the details of my life. My school projects and grades, my relationship with Diane, navigating the personalities and leadership dynamics of my new church community—all things we'd talk about two or three times a week when either she or I called.

"I know you're busy, I just wanted to ask you to pray," she said. Her voice was particularly low even with the wind.

"Pray? What's wrong?" I shouted into the phone. "What happened? Pray for what?" I stopped walking and shielded the phone from the wind with my mitten-covered hand so that I could hear her better.

"Just pray," she said. "And when the Spirit reveals what it needs to, give me a call." Her voice was calm yet resigned.

"Granny, you're not making sense. What do you want me to pray for?" I was startled and confused by this cryptic prayer request.

"Chile, get to class," she said. "Just pray, and I'll talk to you later." We ended our calls with some variation of "see you later" or "talk to you soon" instead of saying, "goodbye".

For the next two days, I was distracted by my grandmother's request, and since I didn't know how or what Spirit would reveal, I found myself whispering prayers or simply praying in my mind for clarity and direction often. Whether I was sitting in English class, milling over Psychology homework, or across from Diane at dinner in our apartment, my mind obsessed over the phrase, "Just pray".

One evening after dinner, I retreated to our spacious basement-level bedroom, closed the door and shades, and lit the candles that were on the makeshift altar that also doubled as a nightstand when I wasn't praying. I sat on the edge of our full-sized bed and opened the tattered, crunchy pages of my heavily outlined black leather Bible.

The book opened to Acts 2, and after reading the entire second chapter, I retrieved the slender vial of lavender scented oil I kept in the drawer of the nightstand. After unscrewing the cap, I dabbed oil onto my fingertip, etched an oily cross into the palm of my hand, then clasped both hands together and kneeled beside the bed.

I closed my eyes and random thoughts about the day danced around my mind. Suddenly, a stillness quietly overtook me, and I entered an in-between space. In this space, there is neither feeling nor sensation, and time is measured only by breath.

Pictures of my grandmother projected through my mind, one after another. When the slideshow finished, the brightest white light with a bluish tint captured my heart in my chest and startled me awake from the dreamlike state. I got up immediately from the floor and called my grandmother.

"Granny, I know it's the middle of the night," I said when she answered the phone. "But I had to call." My heart was racing, and my mind confused.

"Hey baby, you alright?" she said. "It is late." Her voice was clear and sleepy.

"Granny, you told me to pray. I can't explain it, but I know that you're not alright," I began sobbing into the phone. "You're not alright, are you?"

"Baby, I'll be fine," she said, and although her voice was confident, I was not convinced.

"How long do you have to live?" I asked.

"They say it could be 3 months or 3 years. But I'm not worried and I don't want you to worry. I get to go home and be with Jesus," she said, clearing the ball of emotion from her throat.

"Is it cancer?" I cried.

"Nah chile, it's lupus. And my kidneys are gone they say. I'm gonna have to start dialysis," she said plainly.

"Granny, when did you find this out? When do you start dialysis? I want to be there for your appointment."

"I went to the doctor last week. I've been having some pains," she said before pausing to take a sip of water.

"I start dialysis at the end of the week," she continued. "There were some problems with my health insurance but it's all straightened out now."

"What day is your appointment? I want to come with you," I said. Time was suspended, and everything felt surreal.

"They say it's going to last four hours, and I'm going to be tired afterwards. I don't want you there for that. I got a ride set up to bring me there and take me back home. Perhaps you can come over Thursday evening after it's all over and I've had a chance to rest," she said.

"Granny you can't die. You can't," I cried. A mountain of tears flowed down my cheeks as I blinked away mental images of my grandmother in a casket.

"I'll be fine," she said. "You'll see. Now, I'm going to get some rest. Come over on Thursday and sit with me then," she said softly.

"I love you granny," I whispered, through tears and grief.

"I love you too, baby. I'll see you soon."

After I hung up the phone, I sat on the edge of the bed stunned. I knew the day would come when she'd die but I wasn't ready to lose my grandmother. She had become my best friend. I tossed and turned all night, so the next day I decided that instead of waiting until Thursday, which was two days away, I'd stop by my grandmother's apartment after classes that very same day.

After leaving my first class, my cell phone rang, and this time, it was my aunt telling me that my grandmother was found unresponsive in her apartment. I rushed to the hospital to find my grandmother unconscious and on a ventilator. My heart sank into my stomach as I watched her lay there helplessly with machines pumping breath into her body.

Her hair was thin. Her skin was blacker than its normal caramel color, and her eyelids were dark and hardened. The doctor reported that she was dehydrated and had renal failure. I couldn't believe it because I just spoke with her the night before.

Her sterile hospital room was jammed with equipment. A blue curtain hanging by metal hooks separated the space around her bed from the doorway.

She woke up after the second day, and other than not being able to see, she was energetic, lucid and positive—like her usual self.

"Y'all must have been praying hard because I was in my glorified body; this ol' meat suit was gone, and I moved in light," she said, with a wide, toothless grin. The tears in her cloudy eyes were drops the nurse put into her eyes to moisturize them. "A bright blue, nearly white light," she said with excitement.

"Granny that sounds beautiful," I said, standing up to meet her words.

"I can't tell you what it's like," my grandmother mumbled. "You gotta see it for yourself; it was a different kind of being alive. Everything was still, and I had total peace."

"Granny, you don't have a will. No one knew what to do," I cried. "I wanted to pull the plug...we could've killed you!" I blinked hard through my tears.

"That's why I'm back baby... To put everything in order. Take out your notebook," she directed, motioning with a wrinkled hand toward the floor.

"How did you know my backpack was over there?" I asked, my eyes wide.

"I can see in the spirit now!" Granny exclaimed. "Besides, are you ever without a notebook? Since you were 9 and came to live with me, you been writing in a notebook. Ha! Can you believe how long ago that was? You were just a baby…" she reminisced. "It seems like just yesterday. Your hair was all over your head and you were running around barefoot and shirtless in my yard—climbing those trees!" She spoke until her mouth became dry then wiggled her tongue around in her mouth to find any remaining moisture.

"Granny, I'm pushing the call button," I said, "and when the nurse gets here, I'll tell her you're thirsty."

The tears streamed down my face; I had never seen her so helpless. After summoning the nurse, I unzipped my backpack and retrieved a notebook and pen. A presence bigger than both of us entered the room that day.

"When you came to live with me, oh you cried," she said. "You cried and cried. Had me scared to death!" I started transcribing her words.

"You'd wake up in the middle of the night crying and you even got sent home from school for crying. You went to that child psychologist because I knew you needed to tell somebody what happened when you lived with your mom. I never asked you to tell me what happened though, because I knew I couldn't handle it. Even then you were stronger than me," she said, smiling off into the distance. Her voice was a whisper. "Please, stop those tears," she said. "My sun may be setting but your star is rising, chile."

"Granny, you're the strongest person I know. You're the only parent I've ever had," I cried. "You worked hard your whole life and you gave to so many people—even when you didn't have to give. You were unstoppable. You're my hero. Granny, you can't die. I can't do this without you." My heart was breaking in my chest.

Suddenly the nurse appeared. Reality sunk in as she placed a cup of water with a straw and a cup of crushed ice on the adjustable tray table beside my grandmother's hospital bed.

As the nurse checked the machines, I held the cup and straw to my grandmother's lips. She took two, feeble swigs of water before her thin lips released the straw, indicating to me that she had enough.

"We all have to go someday. But I can't leave until you write what I have in my head," she said. "First things first, I heard y'all arguing about what to do. I will sign a 'do not resuscitate'. And bury me in my white dress with my white hat—I laid it on the ironing board next to my hat box when they first told me I was sick." Her brow furrowed as she closed her eyes and started wiggling her tongue around again.

"Granny, stop. I can't do this," I said, as the ink smeared in a trail of tears.

"Come on now, *you are* the strongest. You notice you're the only one here with me, right? It's always been that way," she said softly. "You came to church with me, you went to all those classes when other kids were out there being kids. You got up on that stage with me week after week all those years—reading, praying, speaking."

"Oh my God, all the trips we took," I said, with a smile.

"All those church conferences and continuing education classes. You were always the youngest one in the room. You made me so proud." Granny smiled. "You did everything I ever asked of you. And you're smart. Even after I threw you out on the street like a dog, you have forgiven me. Please, be strong for this too," she said.

"Ok, granny," I said. I took a deep breath. "Whatever you need me to do, I will do it." I gave her more water to drink.

"Help me die with dignity," she said gently. "Write down what I say, my wisdom, and get my kids and grandkids in here so that everybody can hear who gets what so there's no arguing or confusion." She closed her eyes.

"Yes ma'am," I replied. I placed one hand onto her forehead and began gently stroking her hair through my tears.

Each day for three months, I visited her and wrote down what she told me. She shared with me everything from the lessons she's learned and her regrets, to her advice for my life and how she wanted her material items divided amongst the family. Sometimes other people were there with us: hospital staff, family members, or people from the community.

"You know, I worked 40 years and never once saw a sunrise," she recounted one day. "Don't end up like me. I did what I had to do, yes, but I didn't enjoy the ride. I focused on helping and doing, and I spent no time being."

Although her voice and spirit grew stronger overtime, she was losing weight rapidly and she had to wear special cuffs that massaged her legs to keep her blood circulating since she could no longer walk, and her muscles were deteriorating.

"Tell Diane she can have my catering supplies since she likes cooking," she instructed one evening. "Oh, and your cousins Racine and Gwen can have my recipes. Give my suits to your great aunt, Sara—she'd like those," she said.

For the two, sometimes three, hours we visited each day, she went back and forth between directions and advice.

"You got a gentle heart, but don't let nobody take advantage of you," she said one day, her eyes twinkling. "A lot of people ain't gonna like you because of the way you are, but don't stay nowhere you ain't welcome. Life is too short to be miserable. You hear me?" she asked.

"Yes ma'am," I said, observing her intently. I tried to take it all in.

She took a deep breath as I scribbled on the page and said, "and I like Diane, but you need to learn how to stand on your own. God has a special assignment on your life and I can't see it all right now, but your suffering ain't done—you got a lot to do in this world and you need to be tougher, so you can handle it. That might mean y'all ain't together or you're with someone else. No matter what, the Spirit is with you. Some things will hurt but keep praying because you will go places I can't even imagine," she said.

A worn smile covered her sunken face, and just then, a nurse came and inquired about my grandmother's dinner requests. My grandmother always ordered more food than she could eat, because after I fed her, I ate what food remained.

Everyone in the family made their rounds to see her except my dad, who was too drunk and distraught to accept my grandmother's fate. As I was driving home one evening from visiting with her, I was overcome with the same feeling I had when she asked me to pray right before she ended up in the hospital and it had been revealed to me that she was going to die.

I stopped at the traffic light and called my dad and told him that he needed to see her before it was too late. He mumbled that he'd try to make it down as he hung up the phone.

That night, I was unable to sleep and decided to go back down to sit with her. When I got there, she was no longer able to speak. I called family members to notify them and for the ones out of state, I held the phone against her ear as they spoke their last words to her. The doctor ordered morphine, so she could be comfortable.

After everyone was notified, I said my last words to her as I watched her eyelids flutter. I sobbed through each word until I said everything that was on my heart. When I finished crying and telling her how much she means to me, how she saved my life, she mouthed, "I love you."

I touched her forehead and it was cold. I traced the sign of the cross with my finger and I prayed. At the end of my prayer, when I opened my eyes, she mouthed my dad's name.

Not long after, my aunt—my grandmother's daughter and my father's sister—arrived. I told her what happened, and we both agreed that I needed to go get my dad.

When I got to his house, my dad answered the door wearing oversized sweatpants and a dingy t-shirt. His beard had grown, and his hair wasn't combed. After I shared with him that this would probably be his last chance to see his mother, without a debate, he slipped on his shoes and left with me to go to the hospital. Just a few minutes after we arrived, my grandmother took her last breath.

The first three days after my grandmother's passing was considerably easy for me. Unlike the rest of the family, I had adequate time to grieve her departure. The last three months of being by her bedside, processing her words, going through her belongings, and making the funeral arrangements prepared me emotionally and spiritually. Physically, however, I was pushing myself too far to feel anything.

She died on a Friday, and her funeral was scheduled to be one week later. By that Sunday, I was physically drained and running on little sleep. Coincidentally, that Sunday also happened to be Father's Day. I had stopped celebrating Father's Day long ago, however, given the circumstances, I felt compelled to call my dad.

"Hey dad, for what it's worth," I said, as my father answered the phone, "Happy Father's Day." I called him as Diane was driving us home from church that afternoon.

"Thank you for calling," he replied. His voice was tired.

"I also wanted to say, I love you. Things have been rough between us, but I can't imagine what you're feeling right now. She was your mother," I said.

"I love you too. Am I gonna see you today?" he asked.

"Dad, I really am tired. It's been a long weekend. Maybe next weekend after the funeral stuff is over we can go out. I'll buy you a beer; how about that?" I said. I felt guilty that he asked but I was too tired to exert the energy required to visit with him.

Although my father had become friendlier toward me in recent years, we didn't know how to be around each other. And while I offered to take him out for a beer, I knew deep down we wouldn't actually go anywhere.

"Ye'uh…I'd like that. Just you and me—my first born," he said, almost nostalgically.

"Me too, dad," I replied abruptly. "Ok, I should go now, I'm in the car. I'll talk to you later." I ended the call and looked forward to a relaxing evening.

I did have a good evening. In fact, I slept better that night than I had slept in months. The only reason I woke up before my alarm clock that next morning was because of the phone startling me awake.

"Hello!" I shouted into the phone, panicked and anxious.

"Teasha, I am sorry to call so early…" The soft and fragile voice on the other end of the line was my dad's longtime girlfriend, Sandra. She was crying.

The one other time she called in the middle of the night was in the days immediately after my grandmother had been checked into the hospital. At that time, she called because she and my dad had been fighting and she was afraid for him. When I arrived the night they were fighting, the glass in the coffee table in my dad's living room had been shattered and my dad was laying inside the wood-framed table.

That night, as I helped my dad clean the glass and blood, and I listened to the apologetic whimpering from his girlfriend, I remembered my mother and wished that she had had the strength to fight him back when they were married. Perhaps if my mom was able to fight back in a similar way she wouldn't have come after me so much.

Hearing the voice of my dad's girlfriend on the phone triggered me emotionally and sent my head swirling. Had they been fighting again? Was my dad drinking again? Or had she given in and called the police?

"What's wrong? What happened?" I shouted into the phone.

"Teasha, it's your dad!" she sobbed.

"Ok, what happened?" My heart was racing, and I was trying to find my breath by remembering the relaxation exercises I learned in therapy to combat anxiety.

I closed my eyes and leaned my head against the pillow with the telephone receiver nestled between my head and the pillow.

Diane tossed over, but I was hoping that she was still asleep because it would only be a few more hours until it was time for her to wake up and get ready to leave for work.

"He's dead," she said.

The room grew still, and I could no longer feel my heartbeat or hear the thoughts swirling in my head.

"What do you mean he's dead?" I asked.

"Your dad is dead."

I had blown him off on Father's Day plenty of times, but I always assumed I'd talk to him again. I kept my eyes closed and felt Diane sit up. I heard the lamp switch on. "What happened?" I heard myself say.

"We had a great night," my dad's girlfriend said, frantically, "he was so wonderful, and he cooked dinner for me and we made love and everything."

"What happened?" I screamed; I finally caught my breath.

"The paramedics tried to revive him, but they think it was a heart attack. He said he was tired and wanted to go to bed, and when I came in he looked sleep, but he wasn't snoring like he usually does so I shook him. He fell out of the bed…it was like a huge thud. I called 911. Teasha, he's gone," she cried.

"I can't believe this," I said, not wanting to open my eyes because I didn't want to face this reality.

"Teasha, I have to tell you something else, but your dad told me not to tell you…"

"What?" I screamed.

"He already laid out the clothes he wants to be buried in. And he told me that he wants you and your sister, Tanya to have everything."

"What are you saying?" Tears filled my eyes. Diane tried to take the phone from me, but I held onto it.

"When your granny went," she said, "your dad said he didn't want to be here without her and he wanted to make sure he went with her." She now spoke in a whisper.

"How did he do it?" I asked calmly, sitting up and scooting to the edge of the bed.

"He increased his drinking and stopped going to dialysis. He said if he skipped his treatments for a week the toxins and fluid would build up in his body and kill him. His last treatment was 5 days ago—the day right before your granny died," his girlfriend said.

My dad was diagnosed with lupus seven years prior to the day he decided to end his life. He'd been receiving kidney dialysis treatments twice a week since his diagnosis to remove the fluid and toxins from his body since his kidneys weren't able to do this work.

"He killed himself?" I asked, feeling Diane's hand rest upon my shoulder as the tears slowly streamed from the corners of my eyes.

"Teasha, I am so sorry…I promised him I wouldn't tell you guys because he didn't want anyone to stop him," she cried.

I was prepared for my grandmother's death because I had so much time with her at the end. But with my dad, all I could feel was guilt from blowing him off on Father's Day and anger because he didn't tell me what he planned to do.

Part 3. I Am Congruent

Chapter 10: Grace

I didn't have the energy to process my feelings about my dad, so I used my responsibilities to avoid the grief. For the funeral preparations, I just doubled everything that was already arranged for my grandmother, and because my dad had already picked out his clothes and decided what he wanted done with his belongings, there wasn't much prep work.

Unlike my grandmother, though, who had a $5,000 life insurance policy, my dad didn't have life insurance. Thankfully, a distant cousin offered to pay for my father's funeral expenses.

That week, I prayed hard and often as I vacillated between relief and sadness. Was this what my grandmother was referring to when she said that my suffering wasn't finished? I went to classes when I could, and I cried when I couldn't do anything else.

After the double funeral, I spent several days in bed. My grief and being back in my childhood church for the first time since my grandmother told me that I couldn't go back there all those years ago collapsed my soul. The weight of my bed covers was all I could bear. I didn't want to speak to anyone and I longed for the days I spent at the psych ward in drug-induced sanity.

One afternoon, I peeled myself from the mound of covers and decided to sit at my computer to work on my statistics homework. Feeling particularly incensed, I stared at the numbers and symbols on the screen and remembered the graphing calculator I had in high school. *Is any of this worth it?* I thought to myself. *What am I here for?*

Just as I asked myself those questions, a quiet surrounded me. For that moment, time appeared to stop and everything—even the dust—was still. I welcomed the peace, and then suddenly, a small voice within me whispered, "You will make my name great among nations."

The voice startled me, and I shook my mind for clarity. I realized that my hand had been pressed against the keys and my computer screen was covered with several lines of the number 1.

Shaken, I went to the phone and called Pastor Blake.

"Thank you for accepting my call," I said breathlessly into the phone.

"Well, you've been through a lot recently and I just want to support you anyway I can," Pastor Blake said, her voice was familiar and reassuring.

"Pastor, God spoke to me," I said, still sitting at my computer.

"What do you mean, God spoke to you?" she asked.

"A voice inside of me said, "You will make my name great among nations." It was faint but it's like I heard it in my soul," I explained.

"God speaks to us in many different ways and it's for us to discern what it means," the pastor replied.

"What do you think it means?" I asked.

"Pray on it, and I will pray too," she said. "If God gives me the same message God gives you after we both pray, then it will be confirmed."

For the next week, I prayed. In our religious tradition, if anyone felt they had received a word from God, the test to prove that it is in fact God and not our own imaginations is to have more than one person praying in earnest for God to reveal the truth to them. If God reveals the same truth to each person praying, then that truth is confirmed.

I weighed my pastor's words and the wisdom my grandmother imparted before she died against the still, small voice I heard at the computer that day.

During my prayers, images of me standing at pulpits and altars, along with faceless groups of people flashed in my mind. One afternoon, after praying for about an hour, my soul filled with these words,

You are one of my ministers. You will help people freely live as their most authentic self by learning how to live as your most authentic self.

I was so eager to talk to Pastor Blake about what I'd heard in the spirit. At Bible study later that week, I stayed behind to speak with her. The other church members filed into the hall to catch up on one another's lives, and my pastor and I sat down together at the big oak meeting table in the center of the modest-sized classroom.

"Pastor, I've been praying and before I tell you what I think God is saying to me, I want to know what you've been told," I said.

"I've recognized in you the gift," she said boldly, "so I wasn't surprised when you called me." Her smile was wide, and her honest eyes glistened.

"What gift?" I asked.

"The gift of the Holy Spirit. There is no question that God has called you, and in the short time I was able to spend with your grandmother before she died, I know that she also knew there's a call on your life," Pastor Blake responded.

"What does it mean to have a call on your life?" I asked. My palms were sweaty, and butterflies began to rumble in my stomach.

"Let me ask you this—do you love God?" she said.

"Yes, of course I do," I answered. "With my whole heart."

"Do you believe that the power of God is real and can transform people's lives?" she asked.

"Yes. I've walked with God since I was a child and God is the only thing I'm sure of besides death," I said. My eyes filled with tears.

"Then serve God and use your life to share God's power with the people you meet," Pastor Blake said, taking my hands into her hands.

"What do I do now?" I wondered aloud. I was leaping inside myself.

"Every minister has a message," the pastor said tenderly. "Only time can reveal what that means for you. I've contacted the Bishop and told her about you. She agrees it's time you enter lay ministerial training and begin to hone your skills. Can you commit one year to learning?" she inquired.

"Yes, I can commit one year," I replied.

"Classes start soon. I advise you to use this time to think about what God is calling you to do—what your message is. You also might discern that God is calling you to go on to seminary—and that's a few more years," she exclaimed. The pastor's words came fast and spoke right into me.

"There's a lot you will learn in this process," she said. "Don't expect to get all the answers right away. Just remain humble and open to receiving whatever God has for you. There will be pain and there will be pleasure. You will need to learn how to discern the real from the fake, and how to keep yourself in check. This life ain't easy but it's rewarding. Do you think you can you handle it?"

"I can…I must," I said calmly. I'd heard the Voice so clearly. If this was God calling, there was no way I could ignore it.

****

The year my grandmother and father died, my sister, Tanya, who was living with my mother at the time, moved in with me and Diane. She stayed with us for a few months until she moved into her dorm room and started college that fall.

My youngest sister, Rose, still lived with my mother and my mother's new husband. The stayed in a one-bedroom apartment in the kind of neighborhood where kids didn't play outside alone.

Although my mother and I didn't speak, my sisters kept me informed of the details of her life. She and Slick separated; and she remarried a much older man. She worked in retail and panhandled around the city. Although my mother was relatively young for a mom, her mental and physical capacity had diminished over the years, and she had become less self-sufficient.

My cell phone rang one April morning as I was getting ready for work. I ignored the call and after Diane dropped me off at the bus stop, I listened to the voicemail message. It was my mother. When the bus came, I settled into my seat and called her back.

"Hello mother, I am returning your call," I said apprehensively.

"So, I get this letter in the mail saying I must appear in court because of you," she shouted into the phone. "I can't believe this shit!"

"Anything you have to say to me, you can say before the judge," I replied. My nerves were pounding in my chest.

"That's how it is?" she asked, her voice much calmer than before. "This is how it's going to be? I am your mother, goddammit."

"Excuse me?" I shouted. "You're my mother because you gave birth to me. My granny—she's my *real* mother. She was there to put me back together after you and Slick tore me apart," I said, trembling.

"Look, I'm sorry about Minnie. We had our differences, but she did raise you. God bless her soul," my mother said. She sighed deeply into the phone then said, "Sonny, though? Damn I didn't see that one coming. Your dad was in a lot of pain. I can't believe he's gone..." Her voice softened as it trailed off into memory.

"Honestly, I can't believe it either," I said, closing my eyes. I leaned my stocking cap covered head back against the leather bus seat as tears warmed down the sides of my face.

"That man was my first love," my mom said. "The father of my children—"

"Two of your children," I interrupted, "...let's not forget the father of your third child!"

"Me and your daddy had our differences; he was downright evil at times. But I will always love him," she shot back.

"Mom, why did you call?" I asked. I was impatient and uncomfortable, regretting my decision to have this conversation on the bus.

"You can't take your sister from me," she lamented. "I'm sorry about your dad and your granny, but I'll be damned if I give you my child."

"Mom, I live in a house and I'm about to be the first one in this family to have a college degree," I said.

"I've got a job and I'm studying to be a minister. Diane and I can provide a decent home for Rose. She can finish high school and make something of herself," I stated plainly, trying to reason with her.

"No court will allow it—you're a dyke!" she screamed.

"You've spent your life running behind men who beat your head in—I want Rose to learn more than that," I screamed back.

"No court is gonna give her over to you and that woman—you ought to be ashamed of yourself," she said.

"I should be ashamed of myself?" I interjected.

"I know we all got a little bit of gay in us," she said, "but you took it too far. I will do whatever I have to do to keep my daughter from you. Who knows what you'll do to her. It's not natural. Who's the man in the relationship—is it you? You always thought you were a boy," she said. She was cold and unrelenting.

"How dare you?" I screamed. "You know what, I won't give you the satisfaction of responding to you in anger because I am surrounded by people on this bus," I said before taking a deep breath.

I continued loudly into the silver flip phone, "You can think what you want about me, but I have more to offer Rose than you ever could. You are completely unstable, and you can throw in my face anything you want to, but you listen to me: I would never do anything to harm my sisters. Never!"

My blood was boiling, and the conversation left me feeling claustrophobic.

"There's something else you should know," my mother then said. "Your sister is pregnant."

For just a moment, time became still.

"What?" I shouted. I couldn't believe what she was saying to me.

"Yes, I just found out myself. I'm gonna be a grandma! I'm so excited," she exclaimed. I could hear her smiling through the phone.

"Mom, I plead with you. Let Rose live with me," I said. "You can't raise a baby and she sure can't raise one on her own. What will you do? You live in a one-bedroom apartment and you barely have enough money to eat and make rent," the words came quickly. "How can you even think about bringing a baby into your home?"

The news of Rose being pregnant knocked the wind out of me. I had hoped that like Tanya, Rose would have a chance to go to college and make something of herself before starting a family of her own. I became more determined than ever that day.

"Mom, please," I begged. "I have never asked anything of you. Just this once, think about more than just you. Rose can't bring a child into that home. That baby won't stand a chance and you know it."

"What are you trying to say?" she asked. "I do right by my kids. No parent is perfect, but I gave y'all everything I had."

"Is that so?" I said sharply. "Why did my grandmother have to raise me? You are an unfit parent! That is why I am taking you to court."

"You're just trying to get back at me...you always had it out for me," she said, adding a devilish chuckle.

"I couldn't do much before because I was young, but I have help now and I will tell the judge everything. I will make sure you never have an opportunity to scar Rose's baby the way you've scarred us," I said, this time lowering my voice as I spoke into the phone.

"I can't go to court, Teasha. I can't have nobody digging into my life. You know once those folks—and they're probably white—once those white folks get involved, it's all over," my mother said.

"You can make this go away. Give me custody, mom. It's not like you can't see her. Or the baby," I pleaded. "She's a teenager now. Her and the baby could both have a stable place to live until Rose becomes more independent."

We ended our conversation on the bus that day when my stop came, and I got off the bus. We never went to court. My mother gave in. She relinquished her parental rights and signed over guardianship to me. The judge also granted me temporary guardianship of Rose's baby.

****

"Are you going to get that?" Diane asked one night as we laid half-awake in the moonlit room. The cozy, full-size bed was warm and after a long day, I was tired. The newborn we nicknamed, Little K, started crying and his shrieking filled our modest 3-bedroom rambler.

"I know that I need to go, that I am supposed to go," I said, dryly. I blinked my eyes hard and sat up in the bed. "He's probably wet. I will change him, and I am going to make sure that Rose is awake and watching," I said.

Just then I swung my legs to the edge of the bed and got up to retrieve my bathrobe from the hook on the door.

"How do you think she is doing?" Diane asked while twisting the switch on the bedside lamp.

"She is still seeing the therapist. And the social worker is here twice a week to talk to her and visit with the baby," I said.

"But how do you think she is *doing*?" Diane asked. Her long, brown hair was messy, and her lips always seemed redder when she was sleepy.

"She is still like a zombie," I confessed. "She doesn't say too much, and she just sits and stares in space." I closed my eyes to prevent stale tears and I tied the cord of my robe around my waist.

"What does her worker say?" Diane inquired.

"She obviously inherited mental illness from our mother but her worker says that Rose is sadder than anything else," I replied.

"She doesn't believe Rose is a threat to the baby or herself. Rose's brain is having trouble processing everything that has happened. What she went through while living with my mom, having the baby, being a teenager—she's just one ball of thoughts and emotions," I explained.

"How does someone get over things like this? I mean, I know that you also experienced a really difficult transition period when you were a kid and first living with your grandma," Diane said. "You told me how you went to counseling and how your grandma helped you, but that seems like something that may not work for everyone in the same way. Are they thinking of putting her on meds or having her undergo some kind of treatment plan?"

Diane was now sitting up on her side of the bed; she was wrapped snugly in our down comforter. Little K's cries were getting louder, and I was sure even Rose was awake.

"They are definitely going to try meds, but they aren't starting anything until after the baby is a few more weeks old," I said as I moved across the narrow bedroom and entered the hallway.

As a precautionary measure, I decided to stop and use the bathroom first because there was no way of knowing how long I'd be in the room with Rose and the baby.

We told Rose that she could live with us until she finished high school and was able to live on her own. Diane said she could stay until she finished college or trade school. But as I listened to the baby cry while I was using the bathroom and then washing my hands that night, I wondered if Rose would ever snap out of this. *What if she gets worse like our mom did? Could I really take care of this baby long term?*

I slowly opened the door to Rose and Little K's room which was directly across the hall from me and Diane's room. The light from the hallway revealed their wide eyes, both awake and crying. I walked over to the crib and picked up the screaming brown baby.

His diaper was dry, and it wasn't time for a bottle. I pulled him into my chest and held him close. I walked with him, rocked him, and talked to him until he quieted down and drifted back to sleep.

Before putting him back into the crib, I wrapped his little body snuggly in a baby blanket so that he couldn't move. He looked like a burrito. I learned that particular blanket wrapping technique in one of the parenting classes Rose and I took together.

My mother maintained contact with us as much as she was able. A few short years later, her husband called to tell us that her heart stopped suddenly and that my mother passed away. The day she died, I went down to the morgue and made peace next to her cooling body.

Chapter 11: Fit to Be Untied

"I'm sorry to hear about your mom. I know you didn't have the greatest relationship with her, but losing a parent is still one of the hardest things a person can go through." The short, husky woman spoke as she walked toward me.

Nearly 20 years my senior, Sharon was one of about a dozen of us who met together monthly at local restaurants and eateries for spiritual enrichment and conversation.

That night's gathering was in the private dining area of a local pizza parlor. Amidst pizza slices and pitchers of soda, our time consisted of us sharing the joys and concerns of our lives, we read from the gospel of Mark, had a labyrinth finger-tracing activity, and because it was during the season of Lent, we talked about Jesus' 40 days in the wilderness and how his experience might inspire us to journey within.

After our gathering, several of us stayed behind to help clean the space.

As we were stacking dishes and organizing the dining tables and chairs we rearranged earlier that evening, Sharon, now standing beside me, said, "One thing I do know is that life is too short for any of us to be miserable."

Her curly dark hair was carefully combed back into a James Dean look and she wore blue jeans and a pink polo shirt. Her unassuming energy made her delightful personality all the more refreshing.

"You got that right," I said, with a half-smile. "And even with all the strides I've made in my life, I'm still not happy."

I looked past Sharon to see Diane, who was standing by the door fidgeting with her cell phone. I could tell by her eyes and the way she was standing that she was restless and eager to leave. Our family dynamics, general growing pains, the deaths of my parents and grandmother, and my decision to go to seminary put a tremendous strain on our 7-year relationship.

Any time we had alone together, we filled it with others to avoid our mounting resentments. We stopped talking about things beneath the surface—especially my desire for her to be more Christian and her displeasure with my expression of masculinity.

"What else will make you happy?" Sharon asked me. "From what I know of you, you have a nice home, a beautiful partner and sisters you're really close to."

"Looks can be deceiving," I said sarcastically. "Hey, would you be interested in going for coffee or talking on the phone sometime?"

"Absolutely," she replied. "Let me add your number and I will give you a call later." Just then, Sharon whipped out her flip phone and began punching in the numbers I recited to her.

"I look forward to continuing our conversation," I said. I then walked over to Diane to retrieve the winter coat she was holding for me and I said my goodbyes as we made our way out into the brisk evening.

Just as we pulled into the driveway, my cell phone rang, and it was Sharon. Diane was relieved that I took the call. As Diane retreated to the living room to check her email and social media account, I settled into one of the dark wooden chairs at the matching dining room table and continued my conversation with Sharon.

"Sharon, you're kind of butch and you seem so comfortable in your own skin...how do you do it?" I asked.

"It's because I *am* comfortable. I love me; and the way I see it is that people can take me as I am, or they don't have to take me at all," she said right before belting out a huge laugh.

"See, that's what I wish I could do," I replied.

"What did I do?" Sharon asked.

"You're comfortable in your own skin!" I exclaimed.

"And you're not? Could've fooled me," she said. "You're so beautiful. Every time I see you, you're impeccably dressed. Your hair and makeup and nails are always done, and you look like you're comfortable in your own skin."

"See that's just it, I dress the way I do because that's how I'm supposed to dress, but I'm not comfortable," I confessed.

Over the years, Diane and I learned to make many concessions to avoid conflict. I accommodated her wishes by dressing feminine in public and she made a real effort to embrace Protestant Christianity.

"How do you want to dress?" Sharon asked.

"It's more than that. I can't explain it," I lamented.

"Try me," she said. "I've been around the block a few times in my years and I've seen and heard it all...or at least, a lot of it!" Sharon began to chuckle, relieving some of the thickness in the air between us.

"Do you ever feel like a man?" I asked.

"Ha! Me? No, of course not. I mean, would I enjoy being a man, absolutely. If I died and came back as a man, would I mind? Absolutely not. But I am a woman and very contented," Sharon replied.

"I don't feel like a woman," I said, hesitantly.

"What do you mean?"

"Ever since I was a kid, I've always felt like a boy. I mean, hell, for years I thought I was one! I figured if I dressed the part and acted like a female, then one day I'd feel like one. It hasn't happened yet. And it's just getting worse," I said, in a loud whisper into the phone.

I didn't want Diane to hear me over the television, so I got up and went into our attached garage.

"I just don't want to die in my 40s like my parents did and never find a way to feel comfortable with myself," I said, sitting down in one of the lawn chairs.

"So, you've spent your whole life trying to be a girl, but you've never felt like one?" Sharon asked. I sensed the confusion in her voice.

"Yes, that pretty much sums it up," I replied. I felt foolish saying out loud what I had tried to bury for nearly 27 years.

"Do you ever think you could be transgender?" she said.

"What does that mean?" I asked.

"You don't know what transgender means?" Sharon gasped.

"No—am I supposed to?" I asked, suddenly embarrassed.

"You've heard of LGBTQ, right?"

"Of course, I have," I said.

"The T stands for transgender. I suggest you look it up," Sharon said.

We ended our conversation that evening shortly thereafter. I returned to the inside of the house to find Diane still sitting on the couch surfing the web on her laptop with the television on. I retrieved my own laptop and decided to retreat to the bedroom where I eagerly did an internet search of *Transgender*.

The first thing that came up in the search results was a video. In the video there was a series of pictures. The initial pictures were of a baby wearing dresses, frilly and pink. The slideshow progressed to images of a school-age child who looked more like a tomboy. Then pictures of a very feminine woman with long hair emerged. My eyes slowly filled with tears as each picture transitioned into the next. It was as if I was watching my own life unfold. The video ended with pictures of this same person, but now, *he* had broad shoulders, a beard, an Adam's apple, and a male physique.

I'd never seen anything like it before, and I didn't know exactly how this person was able to transform from female to male. I combed through every video and article related to the word Transgender.

After several hours of research, I was stunned. "I am transgender," I thought to myself. I didn't know that there were other people who shared the same feelings I learned to suppress, other people who lived with gender dysphoria. The following morning, I called my therapist, Amy.

"I think I'm transgender," I said, as she took my call that was transferred over from her receptionist. Saying that phrase aloud was terrifying because I wasn't sure what would come next.

"What makes you think that?" she asked.

Amy was a petite blond woman who I'd been seeing for psychological therapy for almost a decade. I became her patient after my suicide attempt and stint in the psychiatric hospital when I was 19. For the first few years, we had weekly visits, then we gradually moved to more self-directed care and I called in for an appointment as needed.

"I did some research on the word and with all the information I've seen, 'transgender' captures everything I've ever felt about myself," I explained. "Every issue I've ever had with my body. My feelings of not fitting. My discomfort with identifying as a lesbian. It explains it all," I said, feeling simultaneously relieved and sad.

I was relieved because there was now a reason behind all those years of struggle, and I was sad because I wish I could've learned about 'transgender' sooner.

"I can't diagnose you as transgender," Amy said, "and it is going to take more than just an internet search to convince medical professionals that you are in fact transgender. If you are really serious about exploring this, I can refer you to a gender therapist." Her voice was gentle and reassuring.

"What's a gender therapist?" I asked. I suddenly became overwhelmed. What door was I opening, and was I ready for what was on the other side?

"A gender therapist specializes in the areas of gender identity and gender expression," Amy replied. "They can more accurately help to determine if you are in fact, transgender through a battery of tests and assessments."

The thought of what a gender therapist could mean for my life was sobering. For the first time in my life there was an opportunity to live everyday as my most authentic self. Until then, I spent so much energy being the girl everyone thought I was supposed to be. This was my chance to just be me.

After my conversation with Amy, I had the phone numbers and website addresses for three gender therapists to try out. I grabbed a shower, got dressed and went downstairs to the kitchen where Diane was sitting with a cup of coffee reading a newspaper.

"We need to talk," I said, excitedly. I went to the cupboard for a coffee mug. "We've been through a lot together and you've supported me through some difficult things. I need your support with this too," I said, while pouring myself some coffee.

"Are you leaving me?" Diane asked. I turned to see tears welling up in her beautiful, brownish green eyes. When she was either sick or frightened, the green stood out more than the brown.

"No, why would you say that? I love you," I said. I walked over to her chair and began stroking her back and kissing the top of her head. "I'm not leaving you," I said, hoping to reassure her.

"Then what is it?" she asked.

I replied to her question with a question, "Have you ever heard of the word, Transgender?"

"Of course, I have—they dress up like the opposite sex and perform at gay bars," Diane said, matter-of-factly.

"No, those are drag queens and drag kings," I said. "They aren't necessarily transgender."

"Ok, then I'm confused," Diane said, with a puzzled look on her face. "Help me out—what is transgender?" she asked.

"Being transgender is more than just dressing in certain clothes. These are people who feel like the body they were born with doesn't match the gender they are," I explained. I then walked back to the counter to retrieve my coffee cup and took a sip.

"Ok, why are we talking about transgender people?" Diane said. Her voice was sharp and impatient.

"I'm transgender," I retorted.

Diane's eyes locked with mine and a look of genuine horror covered her face. "So, you're telling me that you want to be a man?" she asked.

"That's just it, I am a man," I said. "I've always been one."

"If you want to start dressing like a dude, I will still love you," she said. Her voice was shaking.

"It's more than that," I tried to explain. "I don't want to be some butch woman. This long, curly hair; these breasts; my vagina. None of it has ever felt real!"

Diane closed her eyes as I spoke. She held her head in her hands. I continued, "I honestly feel like I've been living in drag all these years. This isn't me."

"You're transgender?" she said. Just then, she got up from the dining room table and started pacing back and forth across the Berber carpet.

"Yes; I am! Just saying it aloud gives me relief," I said. I took a deep breath and tried to exhale for the both of us.

"I don't know if I can deal with this," Diane cried.

"What do you mean?" I asked. I was shocked by her words.

"Teasha, I'm a lesbian. I like girls. If I wanted to be with a man, I wouldn't have been with you," she said.

"If I transition fully and become the man I've always known myself to be, are you saying you wouldn't love me anymore?"

"I will always love you," Diane replied. "...but if you change and become a man, I don't think we can stay together."

She stopped pacing the floor and walked over to face me. I couldn't bear her look of sorrow and grief.

"Diane, I need to be happy," I said. "I start seeing a gender therapist to process what all this means. I need you to be happy, too. What if I go the whole way through and have surgery and everything? There's no turning back," I said.

"I will always love you and support you, but I'm not attracted to men," Diane said.

Now standing in the middle of the living room, Diane and I held each other. We didn't speak; we just cried. We knew our relationship was over.

Chapter 12: Reality TV Star

The breaking up process for Diane and I started out smooth but ended up going south pretty quickly. Diane began to resent me for disrupting our relationship and I began to resent her for her inability to accept it all. Neither of us earned enough money individually to maintain the life we created together, and the growing tensions between us bought little time to form a proper exit strategy.

By the following summer, I was homeless. Well, not exactly. I moved into Sharon and her partner's home office. My sister, Tanya, lived with roommates between semesters at college, and my youngest sister, Rose, moved into a shelter for women with children.

I met with the gender therapist regularly to complete the requirements for my medical transition from female to male, and I also saw it as an opportunity to learn new coping strategies for the changing dynamics in my life.

By mid-summer and a handful of weekly sessions, it became abundantly clear that while not all transgender people want to or need to have medical intervention to alter their physical appearance, I desired to live more physically congruent as the person I've always known myself to be.

A self that chooses medical intervention. Over the next several months, I told my sisters and my close friends about my desire to transition from female to male, and my desire to physically alter myself. The more people I told, the lighter and more unburdened I felt inside.

Around the same time, I met a publicly out transgender man. Up to that point, all the transgender people I knew were only accessible online. His name was Zac and he was a short, stocky man with broad shoulders, chocolate skin and a thin strip of hair that lined his upper lip and hardened jaw.

His gait was intimidating, and his eyes were gentle. We had seen each other in passing at church events and I had most recently run into him at a cabaret performance showcasing the work of performance artist, Gabrielle Civil.

When I first met Zac, I had no idea he was transgender—he looked just like a 'regular' guy to me. Out of the blue one day, I got an email from Zac,

Hi there. I know we've never really talked before, but I've seen you around and I want to talk to you about being trans. Hit me up if you're interested.

I accepted the invitation and set up time to visit with him.

I didn't know what to expect by meeting with Zac, but I felt like this man had the keys to a world that was mine. I rushed through the day's tasks with excitement and drove furiously down the highway into the city to his 2-story, Victorian-style home one sunny afternoon.

My knocking was weak as I tried to be polite in what was a predominantly white part of town. I didn't want to rouse suspicion by being black *and* an outsider.

My anxiety was going through the roof and after what felt like an eternity, Zac yelled for me to come in. The door was unlocked.

As I stepped into the entryway that was cluttered with boxes of old records, I noticed a Jimmy Hendrix album and posters of Malcolm X, Gandhi, and Martin Luther King, Jr that were hung on the living room walls. The couch was covered with books, loose papers, a backpack, and a laptop, so I opted for a chair at the dining room table.

Strewn about the dining room table were more papers and books, clothing items and dildos. Later he shared that the papers he had gathered were from conferences and classes he attended.

Some of the documents explained the differences between gender identity and sexual orientation, and some were research articles on human sexuality and physiological development. The books were thin with frayed corners and full of highlighted passages. Titles I had never seen, like *Stone Butch Blues*.

Zac emerged from the kitchen and offered me some tea, when I declined because it seemed too hot for tea, he offered me instead some beer that he brewed himself. I accepted the tea because I wasn't completely comfortable drinking homemade beer from someone I barely knew.

He sensed my eagerness to learn as he watched me peruse the books and papers on the table, and he began to tell me about his transition process. He was born a woman and in recent years underwent hormone replacement therapy and gender confirmation surgery to become a man. He was guarded yet cheerful as he spoke, as if he'd seen *the* light.

"How do you know all this stuff?" I asked.

"You just figure it out," Zac replied. His smile was warm and the twinkle in his eyes was feminine and caring.

"I mean, how do you figure it out? I wouldn't know where to even find some of this stuff," I said, as I thumbed through the books and articles on the dining room table.

"That's why we're here, so you can begin learning about this stuff. Most of this stuff is information you can find anywhere, you just have to know where to look," he said, while reaching across the table and placing his hand on my shoulder.

"How did you know that you wanted to be a man?" I asked. He removed his hand and the look on his face stiffened.

"I didn't want to be a man, I am a man," he said sharply. I was immediately embarrassed by my question since it had obviously offended him.

He then told me that he has a twin sister and that he never felt like a girl as he recounted memories from their childhood. Some of the memories were painful for him—like constantly being compared to his sister and never fitting in. His awkwardness was familiar.

"Tell me about your childhood; I've done enough talking," he said, as he got up and headed toward the couch to retrieve something from his backpack.

"I want to hear how you came to this conclusion because frankly, I'm surprised that you're trans." Zac chuckled.

"Surprised? Like am I not trans enough?" I asked, offended. His words took the wind out of my sails and in that moment, I felt like a fraud. Was I not convincing enough to this transgender person?

"When I first met you at church," he said, "you were a girl. You had long hair and wore makeup. You were a girl to me and I didn't really talk to you then because I didn't think we had much in common."

"Why did you reach out to me then?" I asked.

"A few weeks ago, I saw you at the cabaret and you looked very different. You had on more masculine clothes and your energy was kind of boyish. So, I thought maybe you're trans," Zac explained.

"I am trans," I responded. "I just started learning about it and I saw a video on YouTube about a guy who transitioned, and I know that it's what I want to do. I didn't know that trans people existed or that there was a reason behind my struggle with gender identity until now. I've always felt like a boy and it didn't really hit me until I was 9 that I wasn't actually born a boy genetically."

"My childhood was hard enough, and I didn't want to deal with gender stuff on top of everything else. I kind of pushed it away. Feeling like a boy was supposed to be a phase I outgrew. I thought if I just act more like a girl, one day I'll feel like one. That never happened," I said.

"Being trans is more than what you see on the internet," Zac said, smirking.

"And you need to start seeing a gender therapist. A gender therapist will help you navigate this process and if you decide you want to go on hormones, change your birth records or have surgery, you will need documentation from a therapist. Talking to a gender therapist will also help you understand that nothing caused you to be trans. There are plenty of transgender people who have great childhoods and there are plenty of people who aren't trans who have shitty childhoods."

Zac asked what my transition goals were as he placed a paper in front of me entitled, "Transgender 101". *Did I want to take hormones? Did I want to have surgery? Am I going to legally change my name and birth certificate?* All the questions and information was more than I could digest but I was grateful for Zac.

The document he placed on the table said that before any doctor would approve me for hormones or surgery, I needed to have RLE.

"My regular therapist referred me to a gender therapist, but what's RLE?" I asked, skimming the page. He giggled at me, causing me to look up and when I met his eyes, they sparkled again.

"See, there's more to being trans than what you see on the internet," he laughed.

RLE is real life experience; and in order to receive medical intervention such as surgery or hormone replacement therapy, there must be a documented history of real life experiences as a transgender person to show that you are in fact transgender in your everyday life; that you do present as a gender that is different from the one you were assigned at birth; and that family and friends know you as the gender you are now presenting as.

"I was never publicly trans until two months ago," I retorted. "I mean, some friends and family know, but in public I've only just recently started presenting as male. Even you were surprised to see me presenting as male when you saw me at the cabaret. I just don't think it will be believable."

"It's not that I was surprised. And you are believable," Zac said. He got up from the table and went into the kitchen. "I was just so used to seeing you as female and you were a convincing female. You're a convincing trans guy too. You just need a little help presenting as a trans male to the general public."

"What do you recommend?" I asked, pushing the papers and books aside and gathering up all the clothing items and dildos that were scattered on the table. My tea had gotten cold and I yelled into the kitchen for Zac to bring me one of his homebrewed beers.

I heard the door to the fridge close and the sound of a metal bottle cap hitting the floor as I studied the clothing items. They looked like corsets and vests. Some brown, some black and some white. Each made from shiny, elastic material. Some had Velcro on the edges, some had a dozen or so tiny hooks that were like the hooks used to fasten bras, and some looked like long bands of cloth. There were also a few jockstraps with tiny pockets in the front of them.

"What are the tiny pockets on the jockstraps for?" I asked loudly while thumbing the material.

"They're to hold your packers and STPs," Zac replied from behind me. He placed a beer on the table in front of me and sat back down beside me as he took a swig from the bottle he was holding.

"What are packers and STPs?" I then asked.

Zac then held up a dildo and placed it into the pocket of one of the jockstraps. He positioned the shaft of the silicone penis downward against the life-like scrotum, and said, "You see these penises? These are packers."

"I thought those were dildos," I said, confused.

"Dildos are artificial penises that can be used for sex. Packers are penises too, but they can't be used for sex because the material is too soft and pliable to penetrate anything—or anyone. You wear a packer to give you the front bulge and appearance of having a penis, but you can't use it for sex," Zac said.

"Well then what are STPs?"

Zac reached into his pants and pulled out a hollowed-out medicine spoon that had a latex tube attached to the end of it. He shouted, "This is an STP!"

I'd never seen anything like it. "What am I supposed to do with that?" I asked, my eyes widened.

"You pee through it. STP stands for 'stand to pee'," Zac explained.

I took a long swig of my beer and it was actually good. Then I asked, "How long did it take you to learn how to pee through that?"

"If you practice often, it won't take long. There are different kinds of STPs— this is one that I made for myself. Not every trans guy even uses an STP, but you'll quickly realize that when you need to pee, and you haven't had bottom surgery, not every public men's bathroom has toilets and if there are toilets, some may not have a door. STPs are convenient because then you never have to hold it in if you have to go," he said.

Zac shoved his STP back into his pants. He told me that I could pick one of the brown penis packers that he had on display to keep. And, if I was interested, he had another STP that he hadn't used if I wanted it.

"Do you have a binder?" he asked me.

"Yes, I have been using an Ace bandage to bind my breasts," I replied. "I saw a guy on YouTube do that."

"I know a lot of guys wrap Ace bandages around their torsos to flatten out their chests," Zac explained, "but Ace bandages are not made for us to use them in this way. You could crack a rib or hinder your breathing. This compression shirt is a binder and it's made to flatten your chest and midsection—and it's a lot easier to wear than an Ace bandage. You can have this one." He handed me one of the corsets that had many hooks.

"Can I put it on?" I asked, puzzled by the garment but intrigued.

"The bathroom is down the hall," he said while pointing toward the hallway.

I grabbed my new penis packer and binder and headed down the hall to the bathroom. I peeled off the plastic casing of the penis packer and shoved the sticky, silicone flesh-like penis into my underwear. I took off my shirt and unwrapped the Ace bandage from around my breasts. I stood in the bathroom and just stared at my exposed self in the mirror. As I put my arms into the corset binder and began fastening each hook, it was like I had crossed an invisible threshold and I was one step closer to receiving the body I always felt was mine.

I put my shirt back on over my binder, rolled up my Ace bandage, grabbed the plastic casing that once contained my new penis and I went back into the dining room where Zac was sitting at the table sipping his beer and reading one of his books.

"How do you feel?" he asked.

"I feel good," I said.

"Are you wearing the packer?"

"I am." The sticky bulge against my flesh felt natural.

"I suggest you go to a sporting goods shop to buy you few a jockstraps with the nut cup pocket in the front because you don't want that thing rolling out," Zac said, holding up one of the jockstraps.

"Where do I find another binder like this one because it's really comfortable?" I said, lifting my shirt to reveal my bound torso.

"I got it online," he said. "I'll send you the link to the website." Zac then scribbled some notes down in a spiral bound notebook.

Zac also told me about a support group for other transgender, Black men that was connected via Facebook and suggested that I join and make connections with some of the other "brothers" in the group. "I'll add you to the group," he promised, as I gathered my things and headed for the door.

I hugged Zac tightly for the gifts of that afternoon, the resources, and the assurance that I was definitely on the right path. He gave me hope and an image of what was possible. And he looked happy in his own skin.

As I climbed into Sharon's green sports utility vehicle that I borrowed to drive into the city that day, I decided against air conditioning and instead rolled down the windows and let the wind blow it's cool onto my face. When I got home, I immediately logged into Facebook to see if Zac added me to the support group. He had, and I began perusing the posts made by the hundreds of guys in the online group.

As I read each post, my heart quickened, and I began to see a life for myself that was well-rounded and full of possibility.

One post that I stumbled upon was an advertisement from one of the guys who was connected to a producer of a reality TV show:

Do you want to be on TV? We're casting a 20-something transgender man of African descent who wants gender confirmation surgery. If you're interested, follow this link to the online application and if you're selected, your surgery will be covered, and you could be a star...

This advertisement was the light at the end of a long tunnel. I applied immediately and within a week, I got a call from a woman representing the casting agency,

"Hello Mr. Richardson, my name is Aurora. Thank you for taking my call. I've read your application to be on the show and I watched your submission video, and I just want to say that you don't look like a girl at all. I showed your materials to my boss and we are shocked that you aren't really a guy."

"I am really a guy. I mean, I'm trans. But I'm a guy. I'm a transguy," I explained.

"You're right. Forgive my ignorance. You see, this is exactly why we want to do the show. We want to introduce America to everyday transgender people and you're perfect. I must say that you're really handsome for being born a woman, but you probably get that a lot," she said. Her voice was sweet.

"Thank you, and believe it or not, this is the first time anyone has ever actually said those words to me," I replied, somewhat flattered.

"I am serious. If I was a lesbian, I would totally date a trans guy," she said, ignorantly. I could hear her smiling.

"I don't actually consider myself to be a lesbian since I am not a woman," I said.

"Oh. How would you describe your sexual orientation?" she asked.

"This is an odd question for me because I've always been attracted to people. I don't really concern myself with whether they're men or women."

"Interesting. Would you say you're bisexual?" she then asked.

"Not really, because that word basically means there are only men and women—two sexes: bisexual—and it doesn't leave any room for people like me who are trans or people who don't identify as any gender at all," I explained.

"Ok, we probably won't lead with that because that's a bit complicated. You are also a minister, right?"

"Yes, I was ordained in 2004," I said. Feeling pressure from being in the hot seat, I got up and started pacing the brown carpeted bedroom I was now renting from Sharon.

"You're so young to be a pastor," the producer said. "You must've known from a young age that you wanted to be a pastor. What does your church say about you being transgender?"

"I am not currently serving a church and I haven't come out to my denominational conference staff yet but the church I'm a member of is totally cool with it," I said. "In fact, there are many trans people at my church which is why I just recently transferred my membership to this particular congregation."

"So, if your conference staff see the show, which they will because it will be huge, this will be their first-time hearing that you're transgender?" Aurora asked.

I was surprised by her question. "If I did the show," I replied, "I'd definitely tell my conference staff that I'm transgender before the show aired. I'm going to tell them anyway because we are in covenant with one another—so it's not a secret," I explained.

"I see, so how does your family feel about it because I know that many African American people—especially the religious ones— have a hard time accepting gay people," she inquired.

"I don't consider myself to be gay, and I know that some folks in my family are having a hard time with me being transgender, but I don't think it's just a *Black* thing," I said.

"Sure. Ok. What about your parents?" Aurora interjected. "Are they supportive? Do you have siblings? What do they think?" Her questions came quick and went straight to my core.

"My parents are both dead and I'm sure if they were alive, it would take them a while to be ok. And I have two sisters, they're both younger. One is ok and the other one is getting there. I think because our parents are gone this feels like another loss. I was their older sister and now I'm not anymore," I went on to explain.

"We could definitely use that!" Aurora said enthusiastically. "Do you think they'd be comfortable on the show? We could have a segment where you tell them you're going to have the surgery and we could film the conversation," she added.

"Honestly, I'm not sure. I'd have to ask them," I said, apprehensively.

"People will resonate with this story. Your parents are gone, and your sisters are having a hard time because they feel like they're losing you too. And you're a pastor so then there's the question of is this a sin or not? I feel really good about this, Mr. Richardson. Or should I be calling you Pastor Richardson? Which do you prefer?"

"You can call me LT. When would filming begin?"

"We are looking to get everything wrapped up in about 6 weeks," she said.

"So, soon, then?" I asked. I was shocked at how quickly they wanted to capture the footage.

"Yes. Will that be a problem? You will have your surgery to be a man and you'll educate so many people on what it's like to be transgender. It will be great! I envision this show as the beginning of a much-needed conversation—especially for the Black community."

"I really have to think about this and I have to talk to my sisters. I need to make sure they're ok," I said.

"We're looking to get this wrapped up soon so how about I give you a call next week?" she said, her voice deflated.

I agreed, and as I hung up the phone, I felt such mixed emotions. In just six weeks, a camera crew could turn my life into a dream in exchange for unlimited access to the most intimate and defining moments of my life. Would anything I said be twisted around to communicate things I didn't intend? Would I be made into a spectacle?

In that moment, I wanted kind eyes and for someone to tell me that it was all going to be ok.

After talking to the producer that day, I reflected on my life, and truly considered all my experiences. The show seemed too easy and too good to be true. Once it's done, it's out there and no one would know everything that led up to my decision to come out as transgender.

I wanted to tell the whole story and I knew that there could be no shortcuts to authentically expressing my journey because after all, we are the result of *all* our experiences.

I turned down the television show opportunity and instead, I took time to learn about myself and time to grow into my new reality.

Chapter 13: What Does the Bible Say?

Having grown up in a religious tradition that places great emphasis on biblical literacy, I knew that I would be engaging many folks who were interested in what the Bible has to say about me being transgender and my decision to medically transition from living as female to living as male.

Gender is a socially constructed term that categorizes people by real or perceived physical/sexual characteristics. The word transgender is a relatively new term that encompasses a multitude of gender identities and expressions inclusive of those identities and expressions that most closely resemble the eunuchs we read about in the Bible.

Eunuchs are people who, for various reasons, live a different kind of sexual reality. Some eunuchs are that way because they are born with ambiguous genitalia. Some eunuchs undergo genital modification and are made eunuchs by others. Some eunuchs make the conscious choice to alter their own physical realities out of a desire to live more congruently with a higher reality.

In Isaiah 56, the prophet lays out the terms and conditions for living in covenant with God. He begins the chapter by saying that to choose what is right brings pleasure to God. In verse 4, the prophet says that even the stranger and the eunuch, who were traditionally looked down upon by the people of Israel, are free to live in covenant with God. In verse 5, the prophet proclaims that God's way of righteousness and covenant is extended to all and their reward will be their reputation and legacy.

In Matthew 19, Jesus tells us that there are some people who are born eunuchs, who are made eunuchs by others, and who choose to be eunuchs for God's sake. It should be noted that in the first part of this chapter, particularly, Jesus also addresses the issue of divorce and offers a word for all those who are *able* to receive it:

Marriage—like any covenant—shouldn't be entered into lightly. If you want to be married, and you follow the way of Christ, then you will enter into marriage for the sole purpose of honoring God—not for any other selfish reason and, as a result, divorce will not be something that you consider easily.

There are some people who cannot or should not marry, or who want to postpone marriage, and for them, their commitment to honor God happens in covenant with the church. In the same way, those who have made themselves eunuchs, who were born eunuchs, or who were made eunuchs by others have the opportunity to honor God through the separation from their physical selves and by adopting the way of Christ.

In Acts 8, the Spirit spoke to Philip—a great missionary for God—and sent him to a place in the desert where he found an Ethiopian eunuch sitting in his chariot reading a passage from the prophet, Isaiah. The man asked Philip to explain the passage to him. Once the passage was explained, and understood, the man received the good news of Jesus Christ, asked to be baptized, and went away rejoicing.

Through the passage of biblical time, we see the progression of acceptance for those who were born eunuchs or who became eunuchs.

In the Old Testament, the prophet, Isaiah spoke against the previously held views and laws that restricted eunuchs from being part of the holy congregation of Israel by declaring that all who seek after righteousness will receive it.

Jesus described the lifestyle of a eunuch as one that isn't for everyone but is indeed the case for some. And in the early days of the church, a eunuch with a great deal of social power was baptized into the beloved congregation of God and it's no coincidence that he is found reading words from the prophet, Isaiah.

To honor God fully with our lives requires the balance between our mind, soul and body, and this balance can only happen through and in the Spirit.

For some, this balance is more easily achieved; and for some this balance is a delicate dance that is achieved by bringing the totality of our physical selves under constant scrutiny and subjection as we aim for congruence.

The existence of someone who is born with a gender identity that is outside the status quo is just as real as the existence of someone who undergoes any kind of physical alteration or separation to become aligned with a different, higher or more appropriate reality.

We are not the bodies we wear; our bodies are temples for the dwelling of the Holy Spirit. And once our physical bodies die and we ascend to a different reality, the bodies that we wear will return to dust. For those who seek righteousness and covenant with God, we cannot be discouraged by those who discriminate against us out of ignorance or by the religious people who use the name of God, and silly posturing, to try and isolate people from the promises of a reality with God.

The Spirit is freely given to us all to do that which inspires the very same Spirit to flow freely from within us. Righteousness is a state of being that follows the way of Jesus. And while it may not be socially acceptable to be anything other than what is popular, God has always and will always honor the lives of those who seek to honor God.

Epilogue: I Know What Heaven Looks Like

One afternoon, I got a call from my youngest sister, Rose. She and her wife now lived in a house with their two sons in the city.

Whenever I returned home from an extended business trip, Rose called to check in on me and to remind me about our next monthly sibling gathering that she, Tanya and myself alternated planning. The upcoming sibling gathering was going to be hosted at Tanya's house because she and her husband just had a baby and she wanted to stay close to home.

"LT—I'm not sure if you want to hear this but my dad is in the hospital and they don't think he's going to make it," Rose said. My sister's voice was calm but its barely audible whisper told me that she had been crying.

"Wow, I haven't thought about your dad in years," I said into the receiver.

My sister's father, Slick, spent time in and out of jail and my mother eventually left him and remarried.

After a time of healing from my childhood pain and being disconnected from my family, Slick faded out of the forefront of my mind. Now that we were adults, my sisters and I only talked about him on rare occasions.

"I try not to think about him but sometimes I still get angry at him. I only know he's dying because one of my other brothers called to tell me," Rose said, coolly.

I sensed the resignation in her voice and asked, "Are you going to visit him in the hospital?"

"Hell no! Not after everything he did to us—after everything he did to mom. He is evil. He terrorized us for years and he's still alive—and mom is dead! He should be dead. I'm glad he's dying, and I hope he rots in hell," Rose shouted into the phone.

"I know it's hard to think about him in any other way, but you can't spend your life being angry with him. You're going to have to find a way to forgive him."

"I didn't call you for you to preach at me, Pastor. I might forgive him in time, but that time is not now. I don't know how you can even talk about him like he's a person when everyone knows he's a monster. I just called because if he does die, I thought you'd want to know," Rose said, her voice softening.

"What hospital is he at—wait, let me guess…" I said.

"Yes, he is at the hospital we all seem to go to. The hospital we were born at and the hospital our mother died at. Why do you ask—you're not going to go see him are you?" Rose inquired.

"I think I might," I said. "I mean, it might help with closure."

"I got closure," Rose said, now laughing.

"I think I'm going down there," I said. My heart was pounding in my chest.

"I can tell you're a minister because you are looking at this from a spiritual perspective. Me, on the other hand, I don't feel any care or pity for him at all," Rose said.

"I just feel like everyone should have their last chance to unburden their soul before they die," I tried explaining.

"Good luck and call me when you're leaving the hospital. I'll be surprised if he even has a soul to unburden."

I hung up the phone and gathered myself. I put on my clergy collar, grabbed my Bible and anointing oil, and headed for the County hospital.

****

"Hello Reverend. My family must have called you or do you work here at the hospital?" the frail, pitiful, pale man said, looking harmless. He had no teeth, his eyes were sunken in, and there was a nurse fiddling with one of the machines he was hooked up to.

"You don't know who I am?" I asked, surprised.

"No, I'm sorry. You do look familiar, but I've been to many churches and seen a lot of priests and pastors in my day. What's your name sir?" Slick asked.

"It's Lawrence," I said. I grabbed the chair by his bedside, then the nurse left the room and closed the door to give us some privacy.

"Reverend Lawrence, it's good to meet you and I'm glad you're here. They say I'm not going to last too much longer," Slick said. His voice was weak.

As much as I had wanted closure, I wasn't prepared to engage him in this level of discussion, so I opened my Bible.

"You know, Reverend Lawrence, you do look familiar. Have I visited your church before?" Slick asked.

"No, you haven't visited my church before, but you do know my mother," I said, looking long and hard at Slick, trying to picture the shrewd and cunning man from 25 years ago. "I'm Debra's oldest child," I said.

A look of panic came over his face. "What do you mean? Debra didn't have any boys," he said.

"I didn't always look this way," I said, standing up. I pressed my Bible into the golden cross necklace on my chest and approached the bed.

"It can't be," he said.

Suddenly, Slick thrust his hand across the bed. I assumed he was reaching for the hospital call remote. This time, I wasn't the one who was afraid. I picked up the hospital call remote and looked at Slick square in the eyes.

"I forgave you years ago," I said. "I could smother you and cut off your air supply, but that would make me just like you. I come in God. I'm here to pray and give you a chance to repent before you die."

Slick's eyes never lost mine, but he didn't move or say a word. I did what I came there to do. Psalm 23 and Isaiah 46 were bookmarked in my Bible. After I read them both, I retrieved the small vial of anointing oil from my pants pocket. I unscrewed the cap and dipped my finger into the scent-free oil as I had done hundreds of times before. This time felt no different. I sketched the sign of the cross on his forehead—his skin was cool to the touch.

Our eyes remained open as I prayed,

God, you know your children. You know us better than we know

ourselves. I ask you to forgive this man for all the pain and

destruction he has caused, and while I don't know what the afterlife

holds, I do know that you hold all things. You hold each of us, and

you are holding Slick right now, too.

Unharden his heart so that he can feel your love, and as he goes to

his grave remembering all that he has done in this life, God, I ask for

your mercy upon his soul in the next. In Jesus' name we pray, amen.

"You must think I'm a monster," Slick said, as I gathered my things

and headed for the door.

"I'm not the judge," I said, "but I won't pretend that I never prayed

for your death. I am not sorry that you are here suffering like this.

After what you did to us, you deserve to be trapped in here with

nothing working but your mind."

"If I'm so evil, why don't you kill me right here, right now?" Slick

said. By the calm in his voice, I couldn't tell if he wanted death or

needed it.

"That would be too easy," I replied, now standing in front of the door. "That would be *too* easy," I repeated.

"You and I are a lot alike, you know…," Slick said. His ashen lips cracked into a smile.

"I am nothing like you," I said, in a loud but still respectful tone. I was offended by his words.

Slick continued, "When I was almost out of high school, me and a buddy of mine were hanging out after school one day. I won't bore you with the details, but my dad walked in and found him and I, you know—together. Man, you would'a thought I stole something the way that man beat me."

Slick began to laugh. His high-pitched, shrill laugh was familiar. "That's why I joined the military," he said, "hoping it would make a man out of me."

"Wait, so let me get this straight… you are actually gay, and because your dad beat you for being gay, you decided to terrorize the rest of the world?" I said. I was shocked and laughed in disbelief.

"It's not that simple. I am not gay. I like women and men," Slick replied. "I was with your mom for years, and whether you believe this or not, I loved her. God rest her soul."

"You loved her so much you beat her numerous times, you tried to burn her to death by setting our house on fire, and you sexually, psychologically and physically abused her and her children. Wow," I said, with a sarcastic tone. "That's love, huh?"

"Look here, nobody's perfect. No body! Maybe if I could've been me...maybe things would've been different," he said.

"You are a miserable excuse for a human," I said, lowering my tone but speaking much faster than before. "If there is a hell, I hope you rot in it. If there isn't a hell, I hope that you always remember everything you've done. There are plenty of people in this world who lived through worse than a beating and what do we do to cope? We don't harm people! We get educated; we go to doctors; we grow up; we commit ourselves to a higher purpose; we heal; we learn to love ourselves; we find community. Whatever pain you experienced as a child is no excuse for what you've done."

"I'm sorry," Slick said. His voice was barely audible.

"You're what?" I gasped.

"I am sorry. I am sorry I was too much of a coward to stand up to my dad. I am sorry that I took out my anger and pain on everybody. I'm sorry I hurt you and your mom and your sisters," he said. I stood there stunned as pity or remorse filled his eyes.

"You know, I always liked you the most," he said. "You've always had a good head on your shoulders. Even as kid, you were beautiful, and you were so smart. Even back then. You weren't like your mother at all. And now you're a man...an attractive man. Boy, if I were younger we could be together..."

"You son of a bitch—," I interjected. "I did what I came here to do and now I'm leaving before I do something I might regret."

I turned toward the door when suddenly, Slick began singing,

One of these ol mornings, it won't be very long,
you'll look for me, and I'll be gone...
I'm gonna walk around heaven all day...

The words to that familiar tune stopped me cold in my tracks. The song Slick sang during or after the times he abused us. I shook off the shock from hearing the song, refusing muscle memory, opened the door and left Slick's hospital room.

Moving swiftly through the halls, I could feel the nerves I held together slowly rising like a ball in my throat. I found my car in the parking ramp in no time. I climbed behind the wheel and buckled myself into the seat. As I put the key into the ignition, it suddenly hit me, *I'm not the little girl I used to be.*

CPSIA information can be obtained
at www.ICGtesting.com
Printed in the USA
LVHW021601120521
687231LV00009B/761